Process Redesign & Management:

BEYOND REENGINEERING

Process Redesign & Management:

BEYOND REENGINEERING

A Guide to Practical Action

DOUGLAS C. MONTGOMERY, PHD

JAMES SIDNEY JOHNSON, CPA

GARY J. FELDMAN, CPA

Windham Brannon Business Advisory Services, LLC
1355 Peachtree Street, NE
Suite 200
Atlanta, Georgia 30309

Windham Brannon Business Advisory Services, LLC
1355 Peachtree Street, NE
Suite 200
Atlanta, Georgia 30309
United States of America

Telephone: (404) 898-2001
Facsimile: (404) 898-2010

Cover design by SpeakEasy, Atlanta, Georgia

Printed and bound by BookCrafters

Manufactured in the United States of America on acid-free paper

Library of Congress Catalog Card Number: 96-60496

ISBN 0-9652178-0-9

Current printing (last digit): 10 9 8 7 6 5 4 3 2 1

Acknowledgments

We would like to thank Harry Peterson-Nedry for his contribution to the book and especially Chapter 5 on Teamwork - People and Creative Skills. His help was invaluable. We would also like to acknowledge our friends and colleagues at Windham Brannon, PC for their understanding and support during the development of this book. Specifically, we want to thank Anne Ockene, Lori Welch Askew and Shelley Skiles Sawyer for their guidance on matters of style and layout, and especially Debi Blaauw for her unyielding dedication, loyalty and enthusiasm since inception of this work.

Lastly, we want to thank our friends and family for their support and their understanding of the commitment necessary to bring this to fruition. This book is personally dedicated to Meredith, Neil, Colin, Cheryl, Katherine, Kate, Debbie, David and Vicki.

About Windham Brannon Business Advisory Services, LLC

Windham Brannon Business Advisory Services, LLC assists clients in identifying management challenges and opportunities, analyzing those challenges and opportunities, and implementing solutions. Our mission is to help clients make substantial and lasting improvement in performance and profitability.

Our team of proven advisors "partner" with client personnel to champion change and improvement in areas of strategy, finance, operations and organization. We are results-oriented, emphasizing data-driven decision making and ongoing performance measurement. We have worked with Fortune 1000 companies with an emphasis on manufacturing, distribution, product development, utilities, health care and financial services. Our services are equally relevant to manufacturing and service organizations and are targeted to any enterprise that must adapt to a rapidly changing business environment, increased competition and customer requirements.

Contents

Preface

"Reengineering is new and it has to be done."

Peter F. Drucker

Much has been written on the subject of business process reengineering in the past five years. Although it has been hailed by many as the savior of corporate America, few managers or business leaders understand what reengineering really is or how it can be used to increase profitability.

This book explains that reengineering is actually a concept used in the quest to improve key business processes. While it holds the promise of significant performance improvement, it entails huge risks. In our opinion, reengineering represents an expensive and disruptive means of changing business processes.

Process Redesign and Management involves a more analytical and scientifically-based means of realizing performance improvement. We promote an objective evaluation of business processes to determine the degree of change needed and the best approach to bring about the change. We also believe that an ongoing monitoring of processes is necessary to continually strive for improvement.

We will explore the need for improving business processes, as well as managing these processes in the future. We will describe issues and obstacles that will be encountered as well as the necessary guidelines. Additionally, we provide the tools and techniques necessary to improve and manage these business processes.

This book is built on the foundation laid by the pioneers of Total Quality Management (TQM), continuous improvement and process control, including W. Edwards Deming, Joseph M. Juran, Walter A. Shewhart, and others. The initiative and foresight of these people created the quality movement in Japan and North America, which has had the most significant influence on business in at least 100 years.

This book is intended to assist you in beginning or continuing your efforts to make business processes more efficient, effective, and profitable. It is a guide to practical action: a handbook, tool kit, and an explanation of the techniques and tricks for addressing the key issues and problems that you will confront.

Contents

Chapter 1: Introduction to Process Redesign & Management

This chapter defines the various terms and concepts used in improving and managing business processes. It will provide a historical perspective as well as distinguish the approaches used by experts in this growing field.

Chapter 2: Process Redesign & Management - A Conceptual Framework

In order to make business processes more effective and profitable, the efforts of many individuals grouped into improvement teams must be focused. Chapter 2 provides a conceptual framework and specific methodology that will guide the improvement efforts of the organization. This framework ensures that all activities are directed toward the same goal.

Chapter 3: Process Orientation

In order to improve a business process, it must first be identified and defined. Chapter 3 explains how to identify business processes and how they differ from the functional or departmental orientation commonly used to describe how most companies are structured.

Chapter 4: Process Activity Analysis

Upon defining the key business processes present in the organization, the process undergoing analysis must be documented and understood in order to identify opportunities for improvement. Chapter 4 describes the tools used to formally define what activities are inherent in the business process and where within the process improvements are feasible.

Chapter 5: Teamwork - People and Creativity Skills

Team-oriented problem solving is the means by which the creativity of many individuals is combined and unleashed. The involvment of people throughout the organization that bring a variety of perspectives as to the causes of poor process performance and the most plausible solution is critical. Chapter 5 explains the art of working as a team and the need for this pooling of skills and understanding.

Chapter 6: Customer Orientation

Unquestionably the most important ingredient of any redesign or process improvement effort is its emphasis on the customer. After all, without the customer there is probably no reason for a business process to exist. Chapter 6 explains this customer orientation and the need to satisfy both internal and external customers.

Chapter 7: Problem Solving and Decision Making Tools

Chapter 7 provides the primary tools used in a team-based problem solving environment, including making decisions as a team. These tools provide the basis for analyzing and improving processes.

Chapter 8: Statistical Process Control

Statistical techniques have been used in manufacturing for quality control and improvement for decades. Chapter 8 focuses on the use of basic statistical concepts in a process redesign and improvement environment. Although many people fear the complexity of using statistics in business, our methods are not complicated and can be useful for most improvement efforts.

Chapter 9: Measurement Systems

Critical to the success of any process redesign or improvement project is the need to base decisions as much as possible on accurate and timely data, not on wishes, hunches or "experience." Chapter 9 provides an understanding of measurements and measurement systems to evaluate process performance now and in the future.

Chapter 10: Benchmarking

Benchmarking is the process of learning from others to improve oneself. Chapter 10 provides the conceptual foundation, methodology and critical success factors for a formalized benchmarking effort.

Chapter 11: Keeping on Track

As with any change initiative, obstacles and roadblocks are inevitable. It is imperative to gauge when the project is about to wander off course and how to regain lost momentum. This chapter explains how to create the optimum conditions for successful Process Redesign and Management.

How To Use This Book

This book has four intended audiences:

❶   Management, which will initiate and support process improvement efforts;

❷   Team leaders, who will guide the teams formed to conduct the effort;

❸   Team members, who will use the tools and concepts outlined in this book to actually do the work; and

❹   Consultants, both internal and external, who train teams in process improvement techniques and who facilitate the change.

This book will serve as the instruction manual guiding each critical step of the process.

Each chapter consists of the following:

•   At the beginning of each chapter, the principles and key concepts contained in the chapter are summarized to facilitate training. These chapter objectives are represented by the target symbol.

- As with any project, the right tools make the difference in getting it done right the first time and minimizing frustration. We have provided you with a number of different tools to assist you in your efforts.

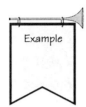

- Examples have been provided to reinforce the tools and concepts. Most of the examples result from the authors' experiences facilitating improvement efforts.

- Throughout the book, exercises are provided to aid in understanding and to reinforce the tools and techniques. These exercises, denoted by the runner symbol, can be performed by either the individual participants or by small groups.

- Also provided is valuable advice throughout the book as to how tools can be used more effectively. Additionally, we describe obstacles that often arise during the effort and how they can be avoided and dealt with. These tips are indicated by this symbol.

- This symbol denotes an explanation of the desired outcome or objective of a tool or a task. It describes what should be accomplished by using a specific technique.

Implementation

The techniques and methods in this book are the result of many aggregate years of experience. Over this time, we have seen countless improvement teams successfully implement these techniques in a wide variety of organizational settings.

We believe that part of the success that organizations have had using these tools is due to our unique approach to implementation. Our philosophy and approach are based on three stages of involvement with our clients.

First, we stress education. Without knowledge of the principles of improvement, no organization can hope to succeed. Dr. W. Edwards Deming stressed the importance of organization-wide commitment to learning these ideas throughout his life, and we firmly believe he was correct.

Second, we always adopt a facilitative role as opposed to a prescriptive one. No outside consultant, however knowledgeable and experienced, can know enough about your organization to completely design and implement a solution to your problems. Effective facilitation and guidance is combined with our tools and methods applied by your personnel to achieve success.

The third component of our approach is consulting on specific technical methods and on problem areas where we have specialized skills or experience.

What follows represents our aggregate experiences and observations, based on many years of working with leading-edge organizations. We hope you, the reader, will enjoy the content as much as we enjoyed putting it together.

> Douglas C. Montgomery
> James Sidney Johnson
> Gary J. Feldman
> Windham Brannon Business Advisory Services, LLC
> Atlanta, Georgia

CHAPTER 1

Introduction to Process Redesign & Management

"We're not going to solve the problems we've created with the same old thinking that created the problems...We need to start thinking differently."

Albert Einstein

Chapter Objectives

Chapter 1 provides a foundation for understanding Process Redesign and Management. We will define our approach as well as:

☞   Explain the other common forms of improving business processes

☞   Provide a historical perspective of process improvement

☞   Describe Process Redesign and Management

☞   Compare and contrast our approach with other popular approaches

☞   Provide the Critical Success Factors to make Process Redesign and Management successful

The Search for Quantum Improvement

Business process reengineering is a business strategy that has attracted widespread interest in management circles. It involves rethinking and restructuring operational processes to achieve dramatic improvements in performance and profitability. Although reengineering has worked for many corporations, its reputation has also been tarnished by misuse. A few companies have reengineered themselves into oblivion.

People are grabbing the idea of reengineering and applying it without knowing for which situations it is appropriate. Many companies are using the notion of reengineering as an excuse to hack away layers of management without first determining which functions add value and which do not.

What is reengineering? What does it mean to reengineer a business process? When should reengineering be used, and when do processes perform adequately?

In 1994, American companies spent an estimated $32 billion on business reengineering. Only 16% of the executives in these companies say they are satisfied with the results while almost 40% express dissatisfaction (see Figure 1-1).

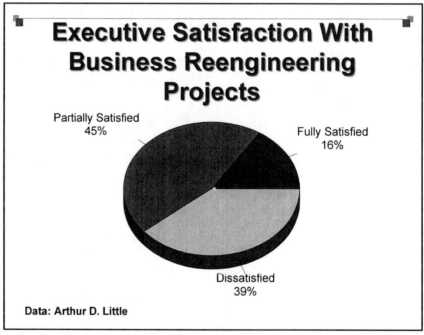

Figure 1-1

Total U.S. spending on business reengineering is anticipated to grow by nearly 20% a year for at least the next three years. In 1997, American business is expected to spend nearly $52 billion on business reengineering. Additionally, about 70% of all reengineering efforts will fail.

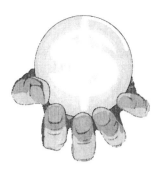

Why is business willing to spend these sums on such a risky proposition? Can the probability of success be increased? Is reengineering truly the best means of enhancing profitability?

One Piece of the Solution

While there is a natural tendency to attribute performance or profitability problems to the people involved in the business or to inadequate information technology, we encourage you to remain focused on the entire business. This "holistic" approach requires that you seek to understand how business processes and organizational designs fit together to form the organization.

Figure 1-2 illustrates this orientation. As you can see, business processes are but one component of a complex and fluid organizational model. The focus of our approach and the others described in this chapter is oriented toward this business process component. While we discuss the other components and their relationship with business processes, this book emphasizes the redesign and management of tasks and activities, and how they come together to form business processes.

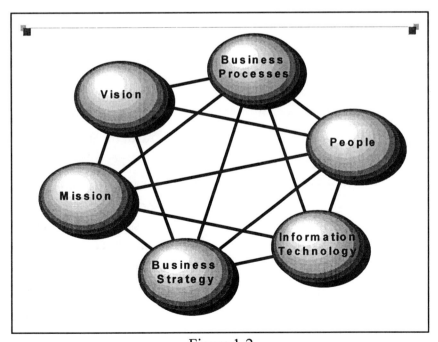

Figure 1-2

It is imperative to consider how each of these organizational areas fit into the overall business model and how they interrelate. To isolate one area at the exclusion of the others would result in unrealized improvement.

Incremental Process Improvement

In the 50 years since World War II, the work of W. Edwards Deming, Joseph M. Juran, Walter A. Shewhart and others formed the foundation for concepts commonly referred to as Total Quality Management and Continuous Process Improvement. The underlying principle of these management tools is that **existing business processes can become more efficient, effective and profitable** by undergoing a structured effort to **eliminate barriers to performance**.

Such an effort to improve business processes is made in incremental steps so as to not disrupt the organization. Also, the effort should perpetuate itself since it can be accomplished by all employees every day throughout the organization.

The following characteristics are common to this disciplined and methodical improvement process:

- Emphasis is placed on **satisfying the needs and requirements of customers** (both internal and external customers). This customer orientation must exist in everything the organization does.

- The barriers to superior performance are addressed and resolved with **team-based problem solving**. Only with the input of all affected parties can the necessary perspective be obtained to make logical decisions.

- **Activities and work steps are standardized** to reduce the opportunity for errors. Further, activities are made less complex by eliminating steps that are not absolutely necessary to satisfy customer needs and maintain quality.

- Management looks outside the organization and incorporates **best practices** when evaluating the performance of the organization. This is commonly referred to as **benchmarking** and involves comparing the organization's business methods with those of leading businesses in all industries.

- The emphasis is on **preventing errors and defects rather than on detection** of these problems after they have been made.

The attractive feature of incremental improvement is that significant success can be attained over time in the way products and services are delivered without undue risk to the organization. Since the fundamental processes currently being used remain more-or-less intact, minimal damage will result if the effort fails. The most significant exposure with this approach is the time and money invested by a company that either chose the wrong process to repair, or waited too long to consider improvement.

The Radical, Clean-Slate Approach

In his article in the July-August 1990 edition of the *Harvard Business Review*, Michael Hammer laid much of the groundwork of a philosophy for radically overhauling business processes. Hammer compared the conventional approach of incremental process improvement to the act of paving cow paths, in that the entire business process should be replaced instead of improved.

Hammer promotes seeking breakthroughs not by improving existing processes, but by replacing them with new processes. He applies the term "reengineering" to this radical, "clean-slate" approach, stating, "Reengineering strives to break away from the old rules about how we organize and conduct business...by recognizing and rejecting some of them and then finding imaginative new ways to accomplish work."

True reengineering is the radical redesign of business processes to achieve quantum gains in cost, service, or time. It seeks breakthroughs, not by enhancing existing processes, but by discarding them and replacing them with entirely new ones.

Simply put, radical, clean-slate reengineering is a high cost, high risk, potentially high payoff effort. As Hammer states, "Reengineering... can't be carried out in small and cautious steps. It is an all-or-nothing proposition that produces dramatically impressive results." Figure 1-3 illustrates the relationship between the effort and stress required in reengineering and its potential return on the investment.

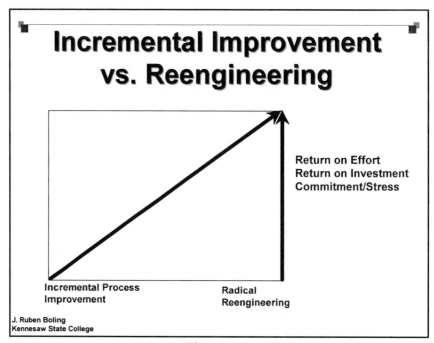

Figure 1-3

Many executives and managers are uncomfortable with the premise that business processes should be scrapped and replaced in a wholesale fashion. Reengineering by this definition is disruptive, expensive, traumatic for staff and management, and offers no up-front guarantee of real improvement.

While most managers have a basic feeling when things could use improving, there are three conditions under which true reengineering **may** make sense for an organization. These conditions are:

- You are experiencing a significant downturn in your business;
- You have recently completed your latest (of several?) reorganizations, and little has improved; or
- Quality of product has deteriorated significantly, and/or customer complaints have increased significantly.

Reengineering is typically appropriate when something has to change in a dramatic manner in order to survive. In these cases, drastic solutions are in order, and an organization is willing to invest in completely rethinking the way it does business.

Most organizations do not fall within this category. While there are always unrealized opportunities for improved performance, the wholesale replacement of key business processes is rarely justified. Alternatively, a less extreme means of enhancing performance is warranted.

Process Redesign and Management

While we acknowledge that true reengineering is necessary in certain situations, its applicability is the exception rather than the rule. Most business processes do not require dismantling. Alternatively, most organizations desire more rapid improvement than is common with the traditional practice of incremental improvement. Our approach offers a blend of these two opposing theories to balance the degree of change desired with timely results and inherent risk.

We believe that incremental process improvement and radical, clean-slate reengineering are the two extremes on a process redesign continuum (see Figure 1-4). They represent the two opposing philosophies of redesign. However, the degree of required process change will usually fall somewhere between these two extremes for most organizations. It is a blend of incremental and clean-slate change that is appropriate for most businesses.

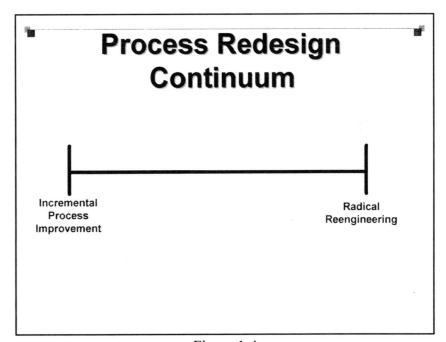

Figure 1-4

Just as each business process is unique, the approach required to bring about productive change must be tailored to fit each individual situation. This requires careful analysis to determine the optimum approach toward improvement as well as the necessary degree of change. Thus, the degree of change needed, ranging from incremental change to radical, clean-slate reengineering, must be considered during such an analysis.

We suggest a balanced approach to business process reengineering rather than dogmatically insisting on either the incremental "tweaking" of processes at one extreme or the "decimate and re-create" approach at the other. The objective of any change effort should be the significant improvement in the ability to deliver quality products and services to the customer. Our approach uses this objective to dictate the degree of change required.

We call our approach **Process Redesign and Management**, or the process by which **continuous or quantum improvement in routine work processes is achieved and the gains made are standardized and maintained**. We temper the idea of "discarding and replacing" with a scientific approach that analyzes how processes perform currently and how much improvement is needed. Our approach seeks the degree of improvement necessary to satisfy customer requirements.

Process Redesign and Management entails:

- Identifying both business processes and their customers -- internal and external;

- Evaluating the performance of a business process via objective data;

- Redesigning the business process to eliminate barriers to peak performance, resulting in enhanced efficiency, effectiveness and profitability; and

- Monitoring the redesigned process in the future to gauge performance and look for additional improvement opportunities.

Our methodology requires a start-to-finish holistic view of the related set of activities that deliver value to the customer.

We use the terms process improvement, process reengineering and process redesign interchangeably

Because this balanced approach results in a degree of required change usually falling somewhere between incremental and radical, **we use the terms process improvement, process reengineering and process redesign interchangeably**. The objective of our approach is to determine the degree of change necessary and to strive to bring about change diligently and prudently.

Though the various process improvement and reengineering pundits may all agree on the end result, this book is grounded on the notion that "starting over with a clean sheet of paper" is often unnecessary and overly risky. It is the reason many recoil at the thought of reengineering their business processes. At least as far as process improvement is concerned, the end should always justify the means and, as with any investment, offer a potential payoff commensurate with the risks involved.

Process Redesign and Management requires that business processes be reexamined from a fundamentally new perspective. A complete redesign of the process may be justifiable or even essential. True reengineering should at least be examined as one alternative to achieving significant process reform, whether it proves tenable or not in the end. In fact, one runs the risks of squelching the kind of creative thinking that the process redesign and management paradigm demands if the following basic question is not pursued: **How might this particular problem be solved if we were starting anew?**

The Future of Process Redesign and Management

The past 15 years have been witness to a proliferation of management fads. From Just-In-Time (JIT) and Manufacturing Resource Planning (MRP) to Quality Circles and Total Quality Management, business leaders have spent countless dollars attempting to become more competitive in an increasingly global marketplace. Unfortunately, the success of these "innovations" has been limited.

Before long, the luster and promise of radical, clean-slate reengineering will be forgotten. Managers will begin looking for the next business salvation. The evangelist traveling the country and spreading the word on the need for radical change, without any advice on how to bring about the change and how to minimize the risks, will begin prophesying on some new quick fix.

Process Redesign and Management is the prudent assessment, improvement and management of business processes. Because many of the tools and techniques described in this book have been utilized in manufacturing for decades, it is reasonable to assume they can be used successfully in a non-manufacturing setting for decades to come.

Our approach may actually represent a second phase of "reengineering." Management is becoming less willing to take undue risk for something as speculative as clean-slate reengineering. We foresee the future of improving business processes as follows:

- **Companies will undertake fewer radical reengineering projects in lieu of efforts that are more thoroughly planned and which reduce risk** by seeking the correct degree of change, not the wholesale "decimate and recreate" attitude of true business process reengineering.

- **Management will demand quicker success.** Many reengineering efforts have taken too long to implement and to gauge success. Those responsible for making improvements must provide some quick success, however small, to justify continuing the investment.

- Process improvement and management will become **more of a continuous effort than a management-endorsed project**. The emphasis will be on establishing ongoing monitoring systems to assess process performance and to continuously look for ways to enhance the business process. These efforts will actually become a component of the business process undertaken daily instead of simply an improvement "project."

- **Companies must regain the confidence of employees who are leery of reengineering's reputation of resulting in downsizing.** Process improvement and management is about more than merely cost cutting and downsizing. It is about becoming more competitive, adding value and meeting all of the needs and desires of customers. There comes a time when the next dollar saved by such practices as downsizing jeopardizes the long-term viability of the organization by cutting muscle instead of fat.

- **Organizations must take a holistic view of the business, beginning with customer requirements**. They must assess their ability to meet customer requirements efficiently and effectively, and consider the human and technological components of the process and how they integrate.

If our vision is accurate, American business will finally approach the point where employees have "ownership" in the processes that they influence and can improve. We will settle into an era in which all levels of an organization are excited and involved in the ongoing improvement and management of business processes that result in delighted customers and increased profitability.

Critical Success Factors

Our experience has identified several factors which are key to the success of a Process Redesign and Management effort. Insufficient time and effort devoted to one or more of these areas usually result in failure or an unsatisfactory outcome. Each of these Critical Success Factors must be considered and anticipated prior to initiating an effort.

Strong Executive Leadership

Strong, committed executive leadership is an absolute necessity for Process Management. Only when senior executives deeply believe in the cause can the organization actually make it happen. Not only the CEO, but the entire senior management team must remain personally and visibly involved throughout the initiative. Efforts lacking strong senior management leadership and participation fail to capture the desired performance improvements.

It is not unusual for the CEO and several other senior managers to devote between a quarter and a half of their time to a successful redesign effort for most or all of its duration. How a CEO and senior colleagues spend their time is a powerful signal to the rest of an organization of the priority attached to the redesign effort.

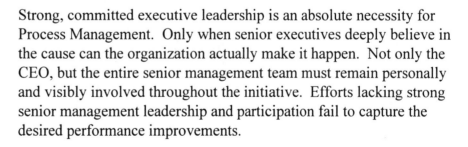

Organizational Goals and Mission

All too often, business leaders have either an unclear vision of their organization's business objectives or there is a lack of consensus among top management on the goals and mission of the business. Without this vision and the strategic operational plan for pursuing the vision, there is little chance that redesigning or managing business processes will prove worthy of the investment required. Prior to beginning any improvement effort, management must know what they want the business to be known for and what the plan is for achieving this goal.

These goals and mission must be communicated throughout the organizaton. Without this foundation, Process Redesign and Management teams will be unfocused and uncertain of their primary objective.

Know Thy Customer

There is absolutely no chance that a process improvement or redesign effort will be a prudent investment unless you know and understand the product and service requirements of your customers. You must invest the time and money to survey customers in order to gain an understanding of the attributes of your goods and services they value. The organization must then respond to this information to better fulfill these requirements efficiently and effectively.

Effective Project Management

Although Process Management involves the continual, ongoing monitoring and improvement of business processes, the early stages of the effort take on the characteristics of a management project. There will be a definite point at which the effort "kicks off" and hopefully a time when the team undertaking the evaluation, redesign and implementation is disbanded and monitoring is conducted by the process participants.

As such, the effort must be managed like any important management project. Meetings should be announced and recorded, target dates established and met, and the status and results of the effort communicated to the appropriate parties. It is imperative that the effort be actively planned and managed.

Six key factors of effective project management are:

- Effective use of teams
- Commitment of time and resources by team members
- Clarity of scope and goals
- Establishment of strong communications
- Realistic planning and schedules
- Effective training and education

Early Project Success

Any redesign effort must strive for a balance between short- and long-term impact. Generally, one-third to one-half of the total performance improvement should be deliverable within the first twelve months of implementation. This initial impact is essential to sustain the energy needed to capture the longer-term improvement opportunities, and to convince management to fund future investments.

Communicate, Communicate, Communicate

One of the most common oversights of process improvement is an under-investment in communication, especially during the early stages. This is understandable given the pressures on the team and the desire to focus on problem solving. Because the redesign initiative is viewed as a change process, it is essential to create a widespread thirst for change, and to generate the energy that will sustain it. This demands an active communication system at all levels of the organization. Without an active communication system, anxiety and skepticism may harden into resistance or even sabotage.

Don't Forget the People

People need some reason to perform well within redesigned processes. Changes that require shifts in attitude are not easily accepted, and merely giving motivational speeches is not sufficient. Management must develop recognition systems that provide the incentive to pursue established goals and objectives.

Many organizations that attempt reengineering fail to consider the impact it has on people. Successful process redesign can change all aspects of a business. When a process changes, so do the jobs of those working within that process. But more than jobs and skill requirements change. The following must also be realigned to fit the new process:

- People's work styles;
- The way they think and behave;
- Their attitudes; and
- What they believe is important about their work.

Set Goals and Use Objective Data

As explained in Chapter 9, it is virtually impossible to ascertain the success of a redesign project without measuring process performance before and after the redesign. The lack of meaningful measurements is the primary reason management often does not understand or acknowledge the impact of a redesign effort.

Measurements should be taken at the appropriate points in the process in order to:

- Aid in determining the degree of redesign required;
- Set the goals of the redesign team;
- Assess the progress of the effort and the ultimate success of the project; and
- Manage the redesigned process through ongoing monitoring of performance.

You have been forewarned and forearmed. There is no legitimate reason for overlooking the fundamental elements of Process Redesign and Management. If you have not addressed these Critical Success Factors or do not feel confident that your organization possesses the ability to satisfy them, do not begin a process improvement or redesign effort - because the chances of it succeeding are small. Adequate consideration of these issues will give your effort a running start.

Conclusion

To achieve maximum improvement, management must look at the macro picture of how the business is run. A holistic view encompassing a process orientation that recognizes the relationship between customers, business processes, technology and human resources is the impetus for quantum advances.

This book guides the organization in redesigning and managing business activities. Businesses must look critically at the performance of their business processes. Most are ripe for improvement since few have been objectively evaluated. Rarely will the solution be the wholesale dismantling of the current process. The inherent risk is usually too high to justify radical reengineering. A disciplined and methodical approach to satisfy customer requirements is the alternative.

CHAPTER 2

Process Redesign & Management - A Conceptual Framework

Chapter Objectives

For any venture to be successful, the effort put forth by individuals, teams, departments and divisions must be focused. The conceptual framework of a redesign effort provides such a focus. This chapter illustrates the elements required for a directed process redesign and management program including:

☞ The Conceptual Framework in which activities are performed; and

☞ A Process Management Methodology for the initial effort.

We strongly believe that each company must develop its own conceptual framework and methodology to meet the unique needs of its competitive environment. The framework and methodology provided in this chapter can easily be adapted to meet those needs.

Conceptual Framework

The conceptual framework is an illustration of a company's continuous improvement model. Each component of the framework builds upon the ideas and principles of the previous component. For example, the first element, vision and mission, serves as the basis for all process improvement activities. Thus, it is unwise to commence work in specific process improvement steps, such as developing measurement systems, if the vision and mission of the process improvement organization are inadequate or unidentified. Components of the conceptual framework include:

- Vision and Mission
- Strategic Overview
- Customer Satisfaction
- Measurements

- Process Definition
- Training and Tools
- Root Cause Analysis
- Process Rating System

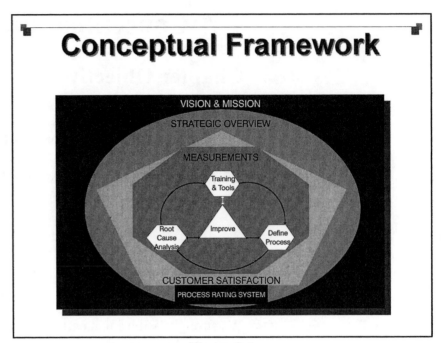

Figure 2-1

Vision and Mission

In today's business world, most successful organizations know how they fit into the marketplace. The corporate vision and mission statement help to create the identity of a company both internally and publicly.

Vision -   1: Something seen other than by ordinary sight (as in a dream or a trance);
2: A vivid picture created by the imagination;
3: Unusual wisdom in foreseeing what is going to happen.

The ideological goal of the entity, and accordingly, the quality and process improvement effort.

A picture of the company's future in its perfect state.

Mission - The written ideology stating why and how the company will achieve its vision.

Together, the vision and mission of a company answer the questions:

- *What business are we in? What is the purpose of this company?* This is probably the most fundamental issue to be addressed for any business. Many companies have not taken the time to objectively identify their product and market. For example, is an office supply company in the business of providing commodities or ensuring that customers are supplied?

- *What will our business be like in five or ten years from now?* If the market for our products or services is changing, how does the definition of our business meet those changes? Can we adapt to an ever-changing business environment?

The way a company performs is highly dependent upon how it defines and directs itself. Vision and mission are global statements of the ideals and objectives of the company that, when effectively communicated, guide the actions of all employees.

Consistency

All activity must correspond with the principles espoused by the mission statement. It is imperative that the goals of a business process redesign effort aid the organization in pursuing its vision and mission. In the most fundamental sense, this pursuit is the only reason a process redesign and management program should exist.

The teams formed and projects chartered must tangibly lead the organization toward its goals. Lack of consistency in purpose and action give the impression that a process redesign endeavor is just another "quick fix" program. The effort should enhance the organization's ability to pursue its mission and objectives.

Strategic Overview

The strategic plan typically guides the efforts of the business entity. In process management, the **strategic overview** is the conceptual plan for pursuing the goals espoused by the vision and mission. Components of the strategic overview include:

❶ Leadership
❷ Identification of Core Processes
❸ Goals of Entity
❹ Organizational Structure
❺ Implementation Plan

❶ Leadership

Quality improvement efforts are generally driven from both the top and bottom of an organization. Management leads, drives and guides the process. Front line employees, on the other hand, have an intimate knowledge of the operations and processes that create the product or services, and are the personnel with the knowledge required to redesign the process.

The program must be initiated and supported by top management in order for the effort to be taken seriously. Corporate leaders should demonstrate active involvement in the initiative by participating in the improvement effort, communicating with key teams at critical junctures, and engaging in other activities that are visible to the rank and file.

Leadership also encompasses the nurturing and advancement of a quality culture and the ideals of the vision and mission statement. Organizations with management support of process redesign efforts progress towards meeting their process improvement goals significantly faster than organizations with only passive executive support.

❷ Identification of Core Processes

Core processes are the major activities that drive the entity. Activities such as manufacturing, research and development, order fulfilment, etc. are often considered core processes. Activities such as accounts receivable, payroll, and data processing are generally considered support activities and are not considered core to the business.

The definition of core processes is always industry or company specific. For example, a company in the information services business might consider data processing a core process. A manufacturer would consider data processing a subprocess, or one that supports the core process of manufacturing. For this reason, the leadership of each entity must guide the effort to identify the organization's core business processes.

❸ **Goals of Entity**

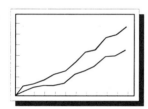

Most companies have quantitative goals regarding performance such as:

- 5% increase in market share
- 10% decrease in operating expenses
- 5% increase in earnings per share

The strategic overview should address the impact of the process improvement initiative on the entity's goals. In addition, the strategic overview should identify specific goals of the process improvement initiative itself. Examples of such goals include:

- Increase customer satisfaction to 95%
- Employee involvement of 80%

❹ **Organizational Structure**

The purpose of an organizational structure for the improvement effort is to guide the improvement and redesign activities. The degree of structure depends upon the entity, its size, complexity and culture. The larger the organization, the more structure that is required due to the size of the undertaking. However, the process redesign effort should not create new or parallel hierarchy that adds bureaucracy.

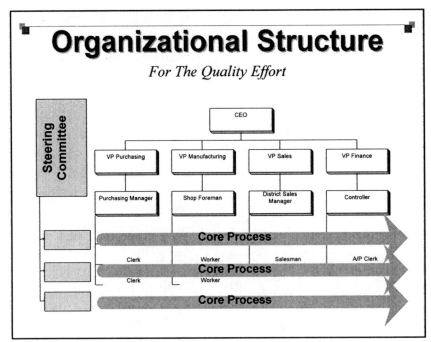

Figure 2-2

Components of a quality organizational structure include:

① Steering Committee
② Improvement Teams
③ Technical Support

① *Steering Committee*

In any process redesign endeavor there must be an oversight function to ensure that goals are achieved and resources are not squandered. The steering committee serves that function. Specific responsibilities of the steering committee include:

- Prioritization of efforts
- Allocation of resources among projects
- Monitor progress of teams
- Ensure balance between short- and long-term objectives

Other responsibilities could include the approval of:

- Formation of new teams
- Implementation plans

Steering committee members should understand and promote the corporate vision and should represent all core processes and all constituencies within the organization. Often the steering committee is comprised of strong performers from different functional areas who bring various perspectives to the project.

② *Improvement Teams*

Improvement teams are collections of individuals who are brought together to solve a particular problem or to improve or manage a particular process.

Teams should be comprised of the most productive and highly respected individuals affected by the process being studied. Too often individuals who have the time rather than individuals who have the requisite knowledge and skills are assigned to a team. Assigning people based only on availability will produce poor results and diminish the perceived importance of the program.

Improvement teams can be organized in various ways dependent upon the size, nature, and structure of an entity. One common format for teams is along the macro and micro processes.

- **Core process teams** are comprised of members from all departments involved in a process and concentrate on the management of a core process.
- **Subprocess teams** work on specific activities and functions of the process identified for improvement by the core process team.

In smaller organizations, action-based teams formed on an ad-hoc basis for a specific purpose may be appropriate.

A **team charter** should be developed for each improvement

team. The charter defines the purpose of the team and can be thought of as the team's mission statement. A charter should identify:

- Processes impacted
- Quantitative goals of the team
- Guidelines for attainment of goals
- Team members

Chapter 5 of this manual discusses team formation, team building and consensus-building tools and techniques.

③ *Technical Support*

Members of quality improvement teams may not have all the tools or skills required to effectively improve a process. Depending upon the size of a company and its experience with process redesign, the required assistance may be available internally or may be sought from outside consultants.

External consultants provide a variety of assistance including training internal personnel, contributing expertise or equipment, or just providing an objective perspective.

We provide Process Redesign and Management services which include training, facilitation and consulting. Each of these services represent varying degrees of involvement by us and client resources. Before committing to a particular outside consulting firm, it is wise to balance the extent to which your team can carry out the project and the resources available for outside help.

Internal support can come from information systems or other departments within the organization. Often individuals who have worked on redesign projects are *loaned* to other teams for their experience and insight. Some of these individuals are trained to become reengineering champions.

A **reengineering champion** is an individual who is a proficient facilitator and has been trained in quality improvement tools and techniques. These individuals often come from the ranks of middle management and have backgrounds in business administration, management, human resources or statistics. Reengineering champions obtain an exposure to a variety of processes and departments and are sometimes being groomed for upper management positions.

❺   Implementation Plan

How will the change to a quality-driven organization occur? A roll out plan with target dates should be established to guide the program.

Pilot programs are commonly used to test the effectiveness of a new process. A pilot program allows a company to implement the changes on a small scale and fine tune the process prior to company-wide implementation

Customer Satisfaction

Companies can boost profits by as much as 100% by retaining just 5% more of their customers.

Some quality experts define quality as fitness for use or ability to meet the needs of the customer. Increasing the quality of products and services will increase customer satisfaction and retention. Enhanced customer satisfaction results in improved competitiveness and profitability. Companies can boost profits by as much as 100% by retaining just 5% more of their customers.

Keys to Customer Satisfaction

Know and listen to your customers. Plan your products, services and activities based upon their needs and desires.

❶   **Customer identification** - Processes have both **external** and **internal** customers. Internal customers are the users of information, services or products within an organization that are generated by a process. Failing to recognize another department as a customer can lead to inefficiencies.

❷ **Customer Oriented Processes** - Determine what your customers' needs are through activities such as Voice of the Customer (VOC) analysis.

❸ **Quality Planning** - Structure your company's product, service, and process planning activities around customers' needs using Quality Function Deployment (QFD).

Customer satisfaction tools and techniques are discussed in Chapter 6 of this manual.

Measurements

Measurement systems provide the information required to move from management by assumption to data-driven management. Over the past few years, Malcolm Baldrige Award examiners have increased the weighting of the linkage between data, management action and the operational and qualitative results.

Measurements provide the baseline information and evaluation criteria with which to evaluate activities. Typical measurements in a business entity include:

- Net income
- Inventory turnover
- Accounts receivable days to collection
- Average days accounts payable outstanding

In a quality-driven organization additional measurements commonly used include:

- Customer satisfaction data
- Process efficiency and variation, such as throughput and errors/defects per unit
- Cost of Quality
- Time and effort devoted to process improvement activities

Measurements can be gathered from various sources using a variety of techniques. The use of sampling techniques to gather information will generally reduce the administrative burden of measurements with little sacrifice in the quality of the information.

Measurement tools and techniques are discussed in Chapter 8 of this manual.

Process Definition

Reengineering and redesign are operational approaches to management and change. Activities are analyzed and grouped into units called **processes**. Each process is a sequence of activities characterized as having:

- Measurable input(s);
- Value-added activities;
- Measurable output(s); and
- Are repeatable.

Processes are defined in various levels of detail dependent upon the current performance of the process and the improvement opportunity. Through process definition, areas of inefficiency can quickly be identified and eliminated.

Process definition provides a clear understanding of all activities involved and helps provide criteria for measurement. Process definition is a key step when benchmarking with other companies.

Chapter 3 discusses methods for defining processes and creating a process orientation within an organization. Chapter 4 describes methods for mapping and charting processes.

Training & Tools

Quality improvement results from analysis and action. All personnel should be trained in the tools used to analyze processes and data. The level of training may vary by degree of responsibility of the employee. Reengineering champions and facilitators will customarily receive the most intensive training. Upper management should receive training in strategic quality planning and change management. Team members should place an emphasis on problem solving and decision making tools.

Chapter 7 provides examples of quality tools and their uses in a redesign effort.

Root Cause Analysis

Errors, defects, poor workmanship, and other indications of poor quality or performance are identifiable. The goal of a process improvement effort is to eliminate these errors and their associated costs. The most effective method for eliminating poor process performance is to identify and correct the source of the problem.

Too often we associate errors with easily identifiable symptoms. Symptoms are obvious attributes of errors, are usually located close to the root cause of the error, and are rarely the real cause of the problem. Root cause analysis can be defined as looking beyond the obvious to determine the events that trigger the symptom.

Root cause analysis is discussed in detail in Chapters 5 and 7.

Process Rating System

Implementing a complete quality improvement program takes time and commitment. Process management is an ongoing activity similar to human resource management. As such, processes need to be monitored and evaluated. A process rating system helps track the progress of the quality effort and the status of the processes being analyzed.

Included in Appendix A is a sample process rating system. In this system all processes are assessed and given a ranking of one through five, one being the most effective and five the least effective. Each process must achieve the requirements of a particular category to progress to the next higher rating.

The categories are as follows:

5. The process is ineffective; major exposure exists requiring expeditious corrective action. The basics of process management are not in place.

4. The process has some operational and/or control weaknesses which require corrective action. The weaknesses and/or exposures are correctable in the near future. The basics of process management are in place.

3. The process is effective and no significant operational effectiveness or control exposure exist. Substantial quality improvement activity is in progress. Process measurement criteria and goals have been established.

2. In addition to Category 3 requirements, major improvements, including simplification, have been made, with tangible and measurable results realized. Business strategy is evaluated with resulting process changes anticipated and committed.

1. In addition to Category 2 requirements, the outputs of the process are assessed by the owner and external users, from the customer's viewpoint, as being substantially error free. No significant operational inefficiencies or control weaknesses are anticipated.

Tips

✏ The conceptual framework for a quality improvement effort is a support mechanism. It is not intended to supplant corporate vision, mission, or principles but to provide assistance through a structured process management effort.

✏ The key factors to keep in mind when structuring your improvement effort are:

- Process improvement is a means to an end, not an end unto itself. The objective is to make business processes more efficient, effective and **profitable**.

- People who understand *the big picture* must lead the effort. This usually means that representatives of upper management must take an active role and serve on the steering committee or its equivalent.

- Change should be made based upon facts. Using quality tools, statistical techniques, and solid quality principles will result in tangible and quantifiable improvement.

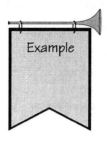

Example

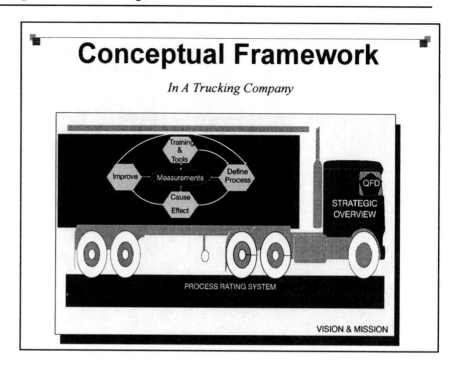

Exercise

❶ Identify the core processes of your business, those processes that are essential to creating the product or service you provide.

❷ Jot down the goals of your company, division or department to be met within the next five years. Is this your corporate vision? Did you think of human resource issues, profitability, new products, market position, etc.?

❸ Does your company, division or department have a mission statement? If not, create one. If yes, does it espouse the ideals you seek to attain in step number 2?

Process Management Methodology

Process management is an ongoing activity without conclusion. Even after significant improvements have been made to a business process, change continues. A competitive business environment requires constant process evaluation and improvement.

A methodology must be developed to continually manage and improve business processes. The methodology serves as the roadmap that guides the improvement effort. The roadmap we promote is not based upon one philosophy for process improvement, nor is it appropriate for all organizations. It is a basic methodology that includes all of the fundamental components for an organized and efficient process management program. With some modification it should be appropriate as a guide for development of an effective process management program.

In any process redesign effort there will be three basic phases:

❶   Assessment
❷   Redesign
❸   Implementation

Whether the process requires change that is radical, incremental, or somewhere in between, all three phases are required.

The three phases and their components are presented in a linear fashion. In practice, many of the activities are performed simultaneously with several iterations. For example, the first component of the assessment phase is the formation of the steering committee. The steering committee will meet periodically as long as process management is being undertaken. The role of the committee will evolve over the life of the process management effort, but its existence is fundamental throughout the process and imperative at the outset.

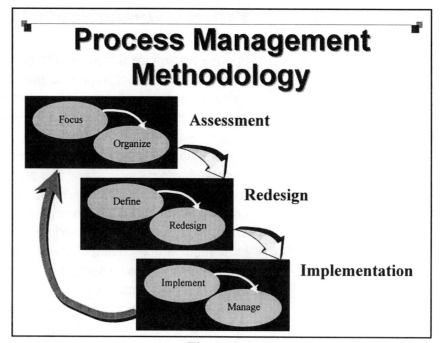

Figure 2-4

Assessment Phase

The assessment stage establishes the strategy for successful process management. One of the key success factors for any improvement effort is adequate planning. In the assessment stage, the organization will create the focus for its efforts and organize the program.

The five components of the assessment phase are:

❶ Steering Committee Formation
❷ Opportunity Identification
❸ Risk Benefit Analysis
❹ Action Recommendation
❺ Establish Work Plan and Schedule

❶   **Steering Committee Formation** - The process
      management program must be guided by the vision and
      mission of the organization. Upper management defines
      these elements, and the steering committee directs the
      process management effort in that direction.

      As the manager of the effort, the steering committee
      prioritizes efforts and allocates resources. In setting
      priorities, short-term gains must be balanced against the
      long-term objectives of the organization.

      Teams are established by the steering committee to tackle
      process problems and improve operational efficiency.
      Teams are formed to meet specific redesign goals. A team
      charter is drafted to outline the goals of the team and the
      approach to meeting those goals.

      The committee also monitors the progress of the teams.
      Committee members may receive minutes of meetings and
      periodic status reports. They may also conduct periodic
      reporting meetings, which consist of team leaders and other
      team members presenting findings, project status and future
      plans to the committee. Committee members then pose
      questions, request additional information and approve team
      plans.

❷   **Opportunity Identification** - At the commencement of a
      program, the steering committee is responsible for
      identifying the areas within the organization with the
      largest opportunities for improvement. These areas will be
      the initial focus of the process management effort.

      The starting point for opportunity analysis is identification
      of the core processes of the business. Once core processes
      are identified, responsibility for the process is assigned to
      an individual - the process owner. The process owner is
      then responsible for determining the greatest opportunity
      areas within their process. He may then request the
      chartering of a team to capitalize on the opportunity. The
      steering committee often uses a criteria form as illustrated
      in Figure 2-6, to determine if the team should be chartered.

Criteria for Projects

To determine if your project will be selected, examine the ten items below.

Yes No

____   1. The project focuses on a definable and recurring process   ___ ___

____   2. The project can be clearly defined. It has both a *starting point* and a *definable conclusion*   ___ ___

___   3. The process is important to the organization and its customers   ___ ___

___   4. The process owner and those closest to the job see the need for a project and want to make the project succeed   ___ ___

___   5. No other teams are currently working on the process ___ ___

___   6. Management is not currently examining this process ___ __

___   7. The Team Charter can be designed to focus on the process *rather than a solution to be implemented*   ___ ___

___   8. Sufficient resources can be obtained to ensure project success   ___ ___

___   9. The process lends itself to data gathering and analysis (The Reengineering Champion can help you gather and analyze measurement data for analysis and presentation)   ___ ___

___   10. Benefits of the project will be worth the effort and are measurable   ___ __

Notes to S.C. _____

_____

_____

Approve ☐   On Hold ☐   Not Approved ☐

Recommendation _____

_____

_____

_____

_____

Evaluated on _____ by Steering Committee

Figure 2-6

❸ **Risk/Benefit Assessment** - The risk/benefit assessment prioritizes efforts to achieve the greatest results with the least resources. For each opportunity there is a risk, and for every benefit there will be a cost.

During risk/benefit assessment the improvement team performs a comprehensive analysis that includes:

- Projected financial costs and benefits
- Potential cultural and/or political obstacles to change
- Potential impact on customer satisfaction

❹ **Recommend Actions** - Quality improvement teams recommend an action plan to the steering committee. The plans should:

- State general nature of redesign contemplated;
- Explain resources needed for project, including personnel requirements; and
- Estimate the projected benefits from implementation.

❺ **Work Plan and Schedule** - Once a plan has been approved, the improvement team develops a detailed work plan and project time line. The work plan is evaluated by comparison with recommended action via monthly progress reports.

Redesign Phase

The process redesign phase encompasses the activities required to improve the business process. This is the technical phase of an improvement program.

The five components of the redesign phase are:

❶ Model the Current Process
❷ Analyze and Verify Models
❸ Establish Baseline Measurements
❹ Redesign the Process
❺ Develop Implementation Action Plan

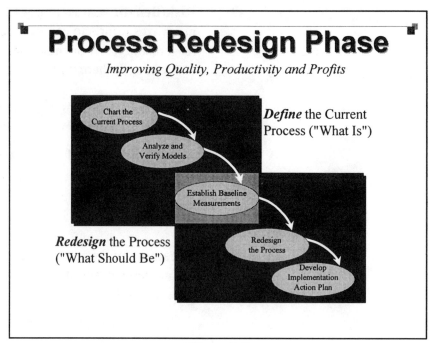

Figure 2-7

❶ **Model the Current Process** - Modeling answers the question, "How do we do this currently?" Process modeling includes process maps and charts which are used to understand the current process and to look for opportunities.

Process mapping includes flowcharting and similar activities with which you may already be familiar. However, we recommend revisiting various mapping and charting techniques to ensure that they meet the needs of a process management environment.

In modeling a process you must take a holistic view. Simply mapping a process without an understanding of how it interfaces with other processes, the customer and suppliers is insufficient.

❷ **Analyze and Verify Models** - Verification of the model is crucial for gaining consensus and ensuring that analysis is productive. Improvement teams post their models and garner input from individuals affected by the process.

Analysis includes:

- Measurement of cycle times
- Determination of information usage
- Functional analysis - "What does this step do?"
- Identification of customer requirements and value-added

During this step, improvement teams identify the key process attributes that affect performance.

❸ **Establish Baseline Measurements** - Baseline measurements serve as the yardstick for improvement. While organizations have many measures of financial and individual performance, very few measures of process performance exist in traditional organizations.

Examples of process performance measures include:

- Response time for a customer complaint
- Cost of processing an accounts payable invoice
- Cost of a scheduling change
- Number of days to close out a month

The improvement teams identify the *critical* measures of performance for the areas they are redesigning and establish reliable baseline measures of performance.

❹ **Redesign the Process** - Answer the questions, "Why do we do this?" and "How can we do this better?" With an in-depth understanding of how the activity is currently being performed and what the critical measures of success are, improvement teams answer these questions.

Using the tools and techniques described in this book, the team can redesign the process to enhance effectiveness, efficiency and profitability.

Implementation Phase

The implementation phase is a critical and often underestimated phase in the improvement process. Determining the best solution for a given problem is meaningless unless the change can be implemented in day-to-day operations. During the implementation phase the redesigned process is tested and adjusted for unforseen complications.

Change is not easy and must be managed. If process redesign results in front line employees being given more latitude to make decisions or a broader range of duties and responsibilities, they must be trained and prepared for their new role. If employees are expected to accept more responsibility, the way they are managed must also change. Managers must become coaches and mentors and will also require training for these new responsibilities.

The five components of the implementation phase are:

❶ Pilot Program
❷ Adjust the Process
❸ Full-Scale Implementation
❹ Measure and Analyze
❺ Refocus Efforts

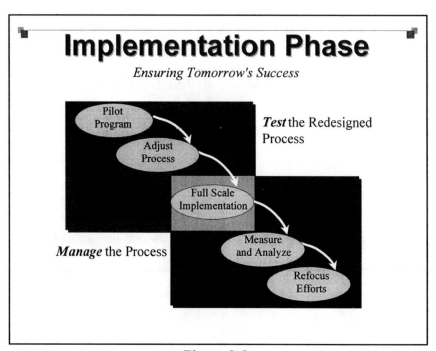

Figure 2-8

❶ **Pilot Program** - Pilot programs are useful to "debug" new systems prior to full-scale implementation. They allow for fine tuning and reaction to potentially unforeseen circumstances. They also provide staff and management confidence in the new program.

Depending upon the scope of the redesign and the extent of the change, a pilot program may be necessary. We recommend pilot programs for any long-term, large-scale redesign.

❷ **Adjust the Process** - Even with careful planning and analysis in the redesign phase, adjustments will be required. Implementation of a pilot program may also allow for additional enhancements that were unforeseen during the planning phase. Processes are often designed for the routine transaction without adequate consideration of unusual circumstances or events.

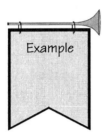
Example

A large utility redesigned its procurement function to drastically reduce the use of purchase orders. A credit card system was devised under which purchasing would be allowed for predetermined items within a specified budget.

Resulting process efficiencies included the elimination of a separate purchasing department, several layers of approvals and summarized billing for the accounts payable unit. Matching of individual invoices was no longer required as the credit limits were pre-determined. Estimated savings were several hundred thousand dollars annually.

A sales and use tax audit was performed shortly after the pilot program was introduced. As the paperwork could not supply adequate information regarding taxable versus non-taxable purchases, the state took the position that all items were taxable. Had the system been implemented as planned, the tax liability could have far exceeded any savings.

❸ **Full-Scale Implementation** - Full-scale implementation may include a radical change in the way an organization does business. Implementation often requires advanced project management skills to properly time and logistically plan for the new way.

Tasks required in a full-scale implementation may include:

- Revision of policy and procedure manuals
- Computer systems modification, hardware and software
- Training for staff and managers
- Development and printing of new forms
- Communication with customers and suppliers

❹ **Measure and Analyze** - Earlier in the process the improvement team has identified and measured the key factors of success for the process. After implementation of the new system, periodic measurements should be taken to gauge the success of the redesign efforts. These measures should also be used to determine what areas could be further improved and what actions resulted in the greatest results.

❺ **Refocus Efforts** - Quality improvement is never completed; it is a road without an end. Using the information learned through opportunity analysis and the redesign effort, the endeavor is refocused on the next "low hanging fruit."

The steering committee should conduct annual planning meetings to set the direction of the program. Lists of high-potential impact areas are developed and scheduled.

Exercise

Think of a process change that occurred in your organization. Write down all of the steps performed to implement the change.

❶ Determine whether additional planning would have eliminated any of the procedures.

❷　　　Identify during which phase of the process the procedures occurred. Think about reordering the steps for better project management.

❸　　　Estimate how much more efficiently the process could have been performed.

CHAPTER 3

Process Orientation

Chapter Objectives

Business process reengineering and quality improvement focus on the **business process**. A business process must be understood and documented in order for it to be redesigned or improved. It is challenging for a team to understand that a business process crosses departmental lines and involves many levels of staff. Such an understanding is essential if improvement is to take place. Chapters 3 and 4 provide a knowledge of how business processes are identified and where in the process improvements can be realized.

Chapter 3 will enable the redesign team to *identify* business processes and process owners. It will focus the redesign efforts on fundamental business processes and not on departments or other organizational units.

Specifically, we will gain an understanding of the principles and techniques related to:

- ☞ Business process defined
- ☞ Process definition
- ☞ Core business processes
- ☞ Subprocesses
- ☞ Process ownership

Business Process Defined

A **business process** can be defined as an activity, or a set of interrelated activities, that transform one or more inputs into one or more outputs intended to satisfy customer requirements.

The characteristics of a business process include:

- An activity or sequence of activities characterized as:
  - ➤ Having measurable inputs;
  - ➤ Having measurable outputs;
  - ➤ Having value-added activities; and
  - ➤ Being repeatable;

- Cutting across organizational units horizontally; and

- Every business activity must be viewed as a process that can be:
  - ➤ Defined;
  - ➤ Measured;
  - ➤ Evaluated; and
  - ➤ Controlled.

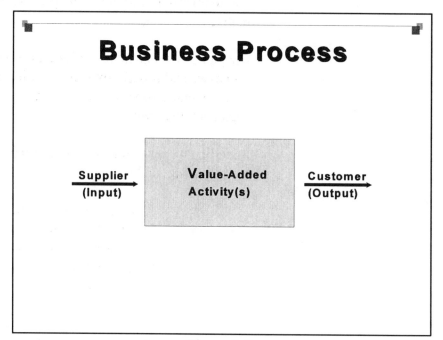

Figure 3-1

Input and output are generic terms to define all products and services required or produced by the process. The supplier as well as the customer may be internal or external to the organization.

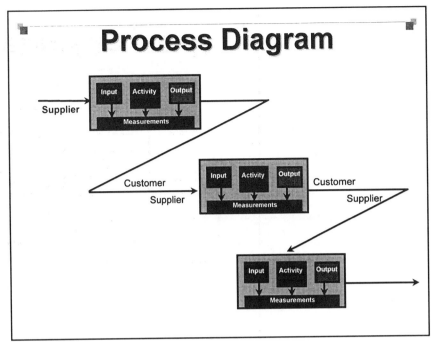

Figure 3-2

Examples of business processes include:

- Product development
- Product distribution
- Procurement
- Inventory management
- Budgeting
- Human resource management

This is only a partial list of the generic processes we might find in an organization. Every organization has dozens or even hundreds of business processes depending on the level of detail used in analyzing the processes. The redesign team must identify the processes that should be improved or redesigned.

Process Definition

The vertical, pyramid-shaped structure of most enterprises is represented in the traditional organizational chart. This structure emphasizes the boss-subordinate work relationship and the organization of people around common functions. See Figure 3-3 for a depiction of this structure.

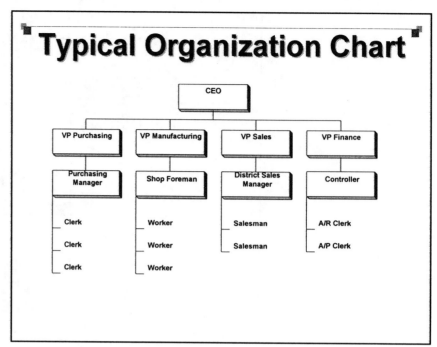

Figure 3-3

In reality, work is performed across the organization in a **horizontal** fashion. For example, in a manufacturing environment, the sales department prepares a request which is sent to manufacturing to initiate assembly. Once assembly is complete, the shipping department packages the goods and notifies the freight carrier of the shipping requirements. Accounts receivable is notified and prepares the customer invoice. These steps are accomplished horizontally across the organization and not vertically within one department or organizational unit.

This horizontal view emphasizes the fundamental work relationship between suppliers and customers, both internal and external. This orientation allows us to concentrate on the supplier/customer relationships and think in terms of the business processes that produce services and products that satisfy customer requirements. Figure 3-4 illustrates this horizontal orientation.

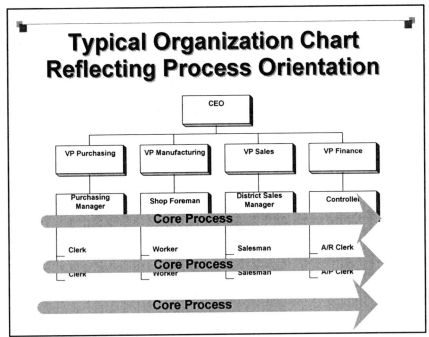

Figure 3-4

Steps in Process Definition

In making the task of defining the business process as thorough and useful as possible, all of the following must be considered:

    ❶   Identify the inputs and the suppliers
    ❷   Identify the output of the process
    ❸   Identify the customers of your output
    ❹   Identify your customer's requirements of your output
    ❺   Identify the process participants
    ❻   Identify the process owner(s)
    ❼   Define the process boundaries

❶   **Identify the inputs and the suppliers**

Input - the materials, equipment, information, people, money, or conditions that are required to carry out the process.

Supplier - the people, functions or organizations who supply the process with its inputs.

❷ **Identify the output of the process**

Output - the product or service that is created by the process; that which is an input of the process customer.

Outputs can be expressed in a noun/verb format - for example: **purchase orders submitted** or **engineering modifications completed**. The reason for expressing the output in noun/verb format is that it forces you to consider both that which is produced and the action taken to produce it. This concept is explained thoroughly in Chapter 4.

❸ **Identify the customers for your output**

Customers - whether your customers are internal or external to the process, they use your output as input to their work processes.

❹ **Identify your customer's requirements for your output**

Requirements - what your customer needs, wants and expects of your output. Customers usually express requirements in terms of the characteristics of timeliness, quantity, fitness for use, ease of use and other perceptions of value. Refer to Chapter 6 for a thorough explanation of this concept.

❺ **Identify the process participants**

Process participants - the people who actually perform the activity within the process as opposed to someone who is responsible for the process, such as the process owner. Process participants can be listed by name or by job title.

❻ **Identify the process owner(s)**

Process owner - the person who is responsible for the process and its output.

❼ **Define the process boundaries**

Process boundaries - the first and last steps of the process. The last step may be the delivery of output to the customer.

Process Redesign & Management: Beyond Reengineering

Core Business Processes and Subprocesses

Core business processes are:

- The large-scale, fundamental processes that represent the mission of the organization; and
- Processes that answer the questions, "Why does this organization exist?" and "What processes fulfill that purpose?"

The customers of core business processes are those who financially support the organization.

Core business processes hold the greatest opportunity for performance improvement for two primary reasons:

- Virtually every department and every individual influence these processes; and
- Since a core business process does not fall within a single organizational area, it has probably not been previously analyzed in its entirety.

Because of these characteristics, one or more diverse, cross-functional teams are best equipped to study it and recommend improvements.

On a more micro level, each core business process is composed of two or more **subprocesses**, often referred to as functions or activities. These subprocesses can be further broken down into tasks, which are executed by people and/or machines (see Figure 3-5).

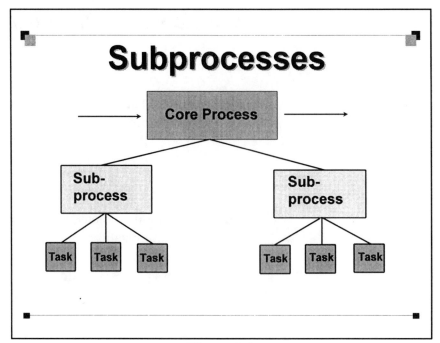

Figure 3-5

Tips

☞ We cannot overemphasize the importance of viewing the organization in terms of business processes. The redesign team must refrain from thinking in terms of vertically oriented departments and áppreciate how activities conducted to meet customer demands cut across the organizational hierarchy. Teams of individuals from the various areas involved in a process (cross functional teams) are best equipped to study business processes.

☞ When identifying the core business process to improve or redesign, ask the following questions:

• Which processes relate to our core business and will be essential to staying competitive?

• What is the primary source of customer complaints? What entire process is responsible for that output?

• Which processes consume the most resources?

- Which processes generate the greatest amount of employee frustration?

- Which processes will be most important in the future?

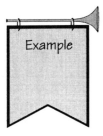

Example

Many professional service firms are involved in gathering and analyzing data, and then reporting their findings. This is usually a core process within these firms and typically consists of other subprocesses required to accomplish each step in the core process. Refer to Figure 3-2 for greater detail.

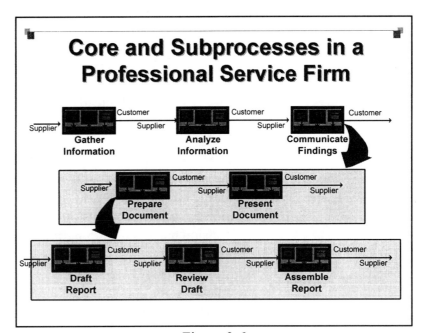

Figure 3-6

Process Ownership

After the core processes are identified, the process owner, who should guide the redesign effort, is designated. A process owner's job is not necessarily to do the redesign or reengineering personally, but to see that it gets done. The owner will oversee the assembly of the reengineering team, obtain the resources that the team requires and gain the cooperation of other managers whose functional groups are involved in the business process.

The process owner has the following characteristics:

- Usually manages one of the functions or subprocesses involved in the subprocess that will be redesigned;

- Has been given the responsibility for redesigning the specific business process; and

- Is typically senior level and maintains credibility and respect within the organization.

These are people whose responsibility and authority reach through the walls between departments. They are ultimately responsible for the daily management of the process, including its input, process activities and its outputs. The process owner is the key decision maker concerning the business process.

Most companies lack process owners, since in traditional organizations people do not tend to think in terms of the business process. Responsibility for processes is typically fragmented across organizational boundaries, with many managers having some degree of control or authority across the process. This is another reason why identifying the company's core processes is a crucial early step in the effort.

Process owners also motivate, inspire and advise their teams. They act as the team's critic, spokesperson, monitor and liaison. Process owners of the subprocesses may be formed into a team that is given the responsibility for the core process.

Tips

☞ We must stress the need to focus on redesigning the fundamental business process, not on departments or organizational units. Analyzing only in terms of organizational units will result in only meager success.

☞ The following are pitfalls to avoid in identifying the business processes to be redesigned:

- **Too many core processes identified**

   Most businesses can be disaggregated into three to five core business processes. These processes have the greatest impact on success. Often redesign teams break down an organization's core processes too narrowly and do not focus on the key performance requirements. If this occurs, organizations are likely to miss major opportunities for improvement and the redesign effort will run a much greater risk of dissipating.

- **Choosing the wrong process to redesign or improve**

   It generally makes sense to select the first process to redesign using the following screening criteria:

   ➤ A process for which the reengineering effort can produce rapid results; and

   ➤ A process that, when reengineered, will result in significant benefit to the customer and the organization.

Process Selection Matrix

A **Process Selection Matrix** is used to identify business processes and to help evaluate redesign opportunities.

❶ Using the following Process Selection Matrix (Figure 3-7), enter key business objectives of your company or department (scope of project) down the left side of the matrix. Typically, business objectives have to do with increased market share, a financial objective, and perhaps an employee satisfaction objective. Others may include safety, prestige, growth, etc.

❷ Separately list the processes for which you are responsible. When complete, ensure each fits the definition of a process. Adjust, revise and reword each idea until there are three to six processes.

❸ Enter your list of processes across the top of the matrix.

❹ Rate each process against each business objective by assigning a value from 5 (process has a very high impact on business objective) to 1 (process has little impact). Work by rows, horizontally. Sum each column.

❺ Two or three of the processes will stand out as having the greatest impact on the business. Using any of the consensus techniques, select one of the processes to map.

Process Redesign & Management: Beyond Reengineering
© 1995 Windham Brannon Business Advisory Services, LLC

Processes → Key Business Objectives ↓	a.	b.	c.	d.	e.	f.	g.	h.
1.								
2.								
3.								
4.								
5.								
Sum →								

Figure 3-7

Outcome

The organization will fully understand the effect each core process or subprocess has on meeting organizational objectives. Process selection matrices help identify the processes that, once redesigned, will result in significant benefits to the customer and the organization.

Exercise

On the following Process Selection Matrix, identify the three to six core processes of your organization (company or department). Follow the steps on page 3-12 and evaluate the effect each process has on meeting every organization business objective.

Processes →	a.	b.	c.	d.	e.	f.	g.	h.
Key Business Objectives ↓								
1.								
2.								
3.								
4.								
5.								
Sum →								

CHAPTER 4

Process Activity Analysis

Chapter Objectives

Chapter 3 introduced the concept of viewing work in a horizontal perspective performed across the organization. We learned how business processes can be defined, that each process should be managed by a process owner, and that core business processes hold the greatest opportunity for improvement.

Chapter 4 expands this process orientation by providing additional tools which allow the redesign team to:

- Document and understand work flows and process activities;
- Begin the search for improvement opportunities;
- Understand where within the business process to utilize the quality improvement tools explained later in this book; and
- Examine and improve the interface between the business process and its suppliers and customers.

This chapter provides an understanding of the principles and techniques of:

☞ Functional Analysis
☞ Process Maps
☞ Process Charts
☞ Functional Business Model
☞ Product Life Cycle
☞ Information Usage Models

Together these are referred to as Process Activity Analysis (PAA) and form the basis for all improvement activities. Regardless of whether a business process should be improved on an incremental basis or is in need of "clean slate" reengineering, PAA facilitates an understanding of current process performance and the degree of change required. Adequate PAA is vital for a successful redesign effort.

Functional Analysis

Functional analysis is a tool for systematically describing and evaluating the tasks in a process with a view toward simplification or elimination. Each object or activity can be described as having a function. In functional analysis the terms **function** and **value** are defined as:

- **Function** - The attributes of an object, product, procedure, activity, service, system, or organization that add value.

- **Value** - The excess of function over cost.

Once function is defined, the value of the activity can be measured and improved. In a manufacturing environment, engineering teams may disassemble a product to evaluate the function of each part. Removing parts that serve no purpose or that can be eliminated without performance degradation reduces total cost and increases the value of the product. The same concepts can be applied to services and business processes. Work activities that do not add value should be eliminated.

Function can be identified with an **active verb and a measurable noun**. This verb/noun combination is important in both understanding the current state and in searching for improvement opportunities.

Evaluation of the function of an activity or object should be kept in context of the process and/or customer satisfaction. Additionally, an activity or object may have multiple functions. For example, a light bulb makes light and generates heat as well. Depending on the environment, the amount of heat generated may or may not be of value to the customer.

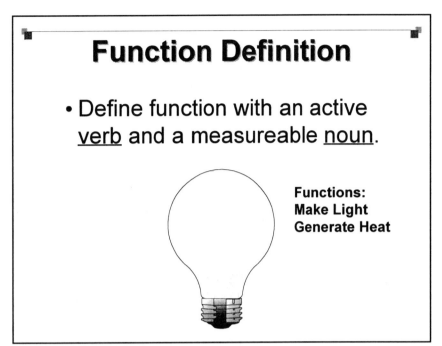

Figure 4-1

Exercise

For the following list of common items, indicate the basic function for each in terms of a verb and noun combination.

What is the **basic function** of:

	Function	
	Verb	**Noun**
1. Pencil Sharpener		
2. Thermostat		
3. Suitcase		
4. Copy Machine		
5. Computer		
6. Copyright		
7. Circuits		

8. Packaging		
9. Printer		
10. Switch		
11. Credit Approval		
12. Automatic Credit Card Reader		
13.Newspaper Editorial		
14. Physical Inventory Count		

Table 4-1

Process Maps and Charts

Process maps and charts are graphic representations of a process showing the sequence of tasks. Documenting processes in this way helps to identify redundancies, inefficiencies, misunderstandings, delays, inspection steps and other nonvalue-added activities.

Process maps and charts help us picture the work itself and not the organizational hierarchy or functions. The goal is to identify the actual path a process follows, as opposed to the one determined without an adequate process orientation.

Process maps and charts are both tools that help you understand and evaluate processes. However, these tools are distinctly different.

- **Process maps** focus on inputs, outputs, and transfers between organizations or departments. They document the general flow within a core business process or subprocess, but do not detail the flow of work. Therefore, they are of a macro orientation and do not contain typical flowchart symbols. Process maps are generally the highest level of detail used and serve as the basis for more detailed process charts.

- **Process charts** focus on understanding the sequential flow of work within a process. They show physical and information flows and are typically used to understand subprocesses. Process charts are of a micro orientation.

Process maps

A Process map is a picture of how a business process functions within an organization. A Process map is used to help understand the organizational "handoffs" within a core process. A Process map shows:

- The process participants;
- The initial inputs and final outputs of the entire process;
- The general steps or activities within a process; and
- The organizations that provide interim inputs to, and receive outputs of, each step (if they are not within the process).

Steps in Creating a Process Map

❶   Determine inputs and outputs
❷   Identify sequence
❸   Draw the map

❶   **Determine inputs and outputs**

Before drawing a Process map, determine what **inputs** initiate the process and what **outputs** end the process. Typically, a process begins with a customer request and ends with an output to the customer.

❷   **Identify sequence**

After completing these initial activities:

①   Identify the sequence of steps; and

②   Identify the inputs/suppliers and the outputs/destinations for each step.

❸ **Draw the map**

① List the process participants or organizations down the left-hand column.

② Show the customer as the first process participant.

③ Draw the activities or steps as follows:

- Horizontally, place them in chronological sequence; and
- Vertically, place them in line with the organization performing that step.

④ If two steps are completed at the same time, draw them in parallel (i.e., the same column).

⑤ Number the steps according to their chronological sequence.

⑥ Connect each step with a line to represent the flow of activity.

⑦ Where there are multiple participants of a step, draw all except the primary participant with a shaded box.

⑧ Identify inputs or outputs that occur during the process but are outside the process. Inputs from organizations outside the process should be shown in the row above the process box while outputs outside the process should be shown in the row below the process box.

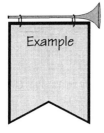

Figure 4-2 illustrates the use of a process map to understand the flow of a customer complaint within an organization. This map depicts the general flow within the process and reflects the various personnel involved in responding to the complaint. Note that it does not contain symbols used in traditional flowcharting. Upon completion of this map, the team can illustrate greater process detail by using a process chart.

Example of a Process Map
Customer Complaint Response Process

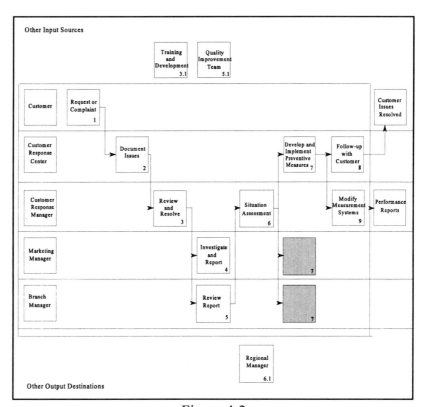

Figure 4-2

Process Charts

Process charts, also referred to as **flowcharts**, are the visual representation of information or physical items moving through a business process. They represent the greatest level of detail in documenting a business process. Using a standard set of symbols, process charts show the sequential activities that occur in a process. Flowcharts are typically used to:

- Understand how an existing activity is performed;
- Investigate where and why bottlenecks or errors occur in a process and where opportunities exist; and
- Help design a new process.

Standard Symbols

When drawing a process flowchart, standard symbols should be established for use during the effort. The following symbols are those developed by the American National Standard Institute (ANSI) and are appropriate for this purpose:

Symbol	Label	Meaning
	Operation	Depicts a subprocess that receives one or more inputs and then transforms the input(s) in some manner to produce one or more outputs.
	Decision Point	A process flowing into this symbol indicates that a decision is necessary in order to determine into which one, two, or three paths the process will branch.
	Paper document	Used when it is necessary to represent a hard-copy document, such as a report, a letter, a requisition form, or a purchase order.
	Delay	Depicts a temporary delay in the process, such as when documents are backlogged while waiting approval or when work becomes tied up due to bottlenecks.

Table 4-2

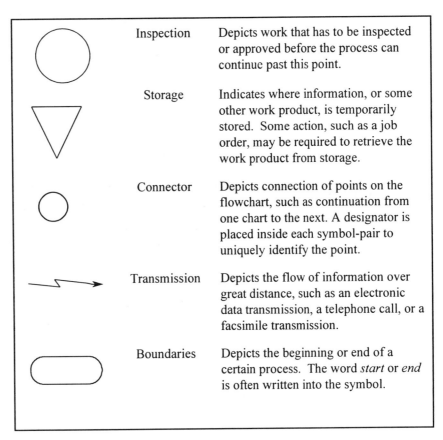

○	Inspection	Depicts work that has to be inspected or approved before the process can continue past this point.
▽	Storage	Indicates where information, or some other work product, is temporarily stored. Some action, such as a job order, may be required to retrieve the work product from storage.
○	Connector	Depicts connection of points on the flowchart, such as continuation from one chart to the next. A designator is placed inside each symbol-pair to uniquely identify the point.
⟿	Transmission	Depicts the flow of information over great distance, such as an electronic data transmission, a telephone call, or a facsimile transmission.
▭	Boundaries	Depicts the beginning or end of a certain process. The word *start* or *end* is often written into the symbol.

Table 4-2 Continued

Steps in Creating a Process Chart

To draw a process chart, follow these steps:

❶ Identify the activities in a process;

❷ Match the activities in the description with appropriate flowchart symbols;

❸ Draw the symbols in the sequence they occur, top to bottom and left to right;

❹ List each symbol with a clear description of the activity. Limit the description to as few words as possible. Strive for using only a verb-noun combination (i.e., "complete form" or "request supplies");

❺ Connect each symbol with arrows to indicate the direction of the flow. Only one arrow typically leaves an activity box while more than one arrow must always exit from a decision symbol; then

❻ Title the chart and review it for accuracy and completeness.

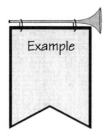

Example

Process charting is not a scientific process. The keys to successful charting include clarity and consistency in establishing descriptions and symbols.

The following three examples demonstrate various forms of charting that illustrate the same business process, expense report processing. These charting methods can be used sequentially to achieve greater detail and understanding of a process, culminating in Figure 4-5 on page 4-13 which reflects the greatest level of detail.

Process Chart - Expense Report Processing

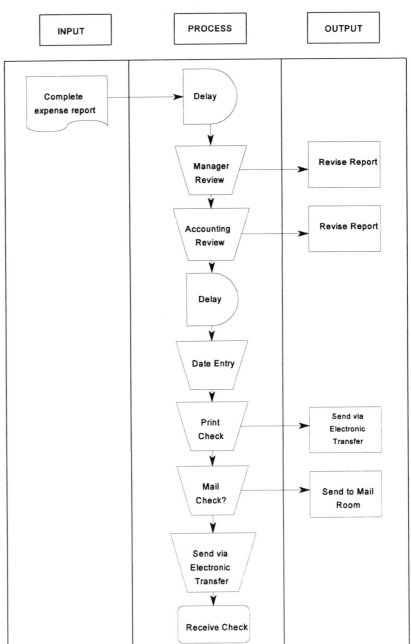

Figure 4-3

Process Chart - Expense Report Processing

Present Method ☐ Proposed Method ☐			**Process Chart**			
SUBJECT CHARTED _____			DATE _____			
_____			CHART BY _____			
_____			CHART NO. _____			
DEPARTMENT _____			SHEET NO. ___ OF ___			

Time in Mins.	Chart Symbols						Process Description
	⬤	○	▭	☐	▷	◇	Expense Incurred
	▭	○	▭	☐	◗	◇	Delay - Sits in Manager's in-basket
60	▭	○	▭	■	▷	◇	Complete Expense
5	▭	○	◤	☐	▷	◇	Submit Report
10	▭	○	▭	■	▷	◇	Revise Report
15	▭	●	▭	☐	▷	◇	Manager Review
5	▭	○	▭	☐	▷	◆	Approval?
20	▭	●	▭	☐	▷	◇	Accounting Review
10	▭	○	▭	■	▷	◇	Revise Report
	▭	○	▭	☐	◗	◇	Delay - Sits in Data Entry area
	▭	○	▭	☐	▷	◆	Allowable Expense?
10	▭	○	▭	■	▷	◇	Data Entry
10	▭	○	▭	☐	▷	◆	Math Errors?
10	▭	○	▭	■	▷	◇	Print Check
	▭	○	▭	☐	▷	◆	Mail Check?
15	▭	○	▭	■	▷	◇	Send via Electronic
	▭	●	▭	☐	▷	◇	Send to Mail Room
	⬤	○	▭	☐	▷	◇	Receive Check
170		3	1	6	2	4	Total

Figure 4-4

Process Chart - Expense Report Processing

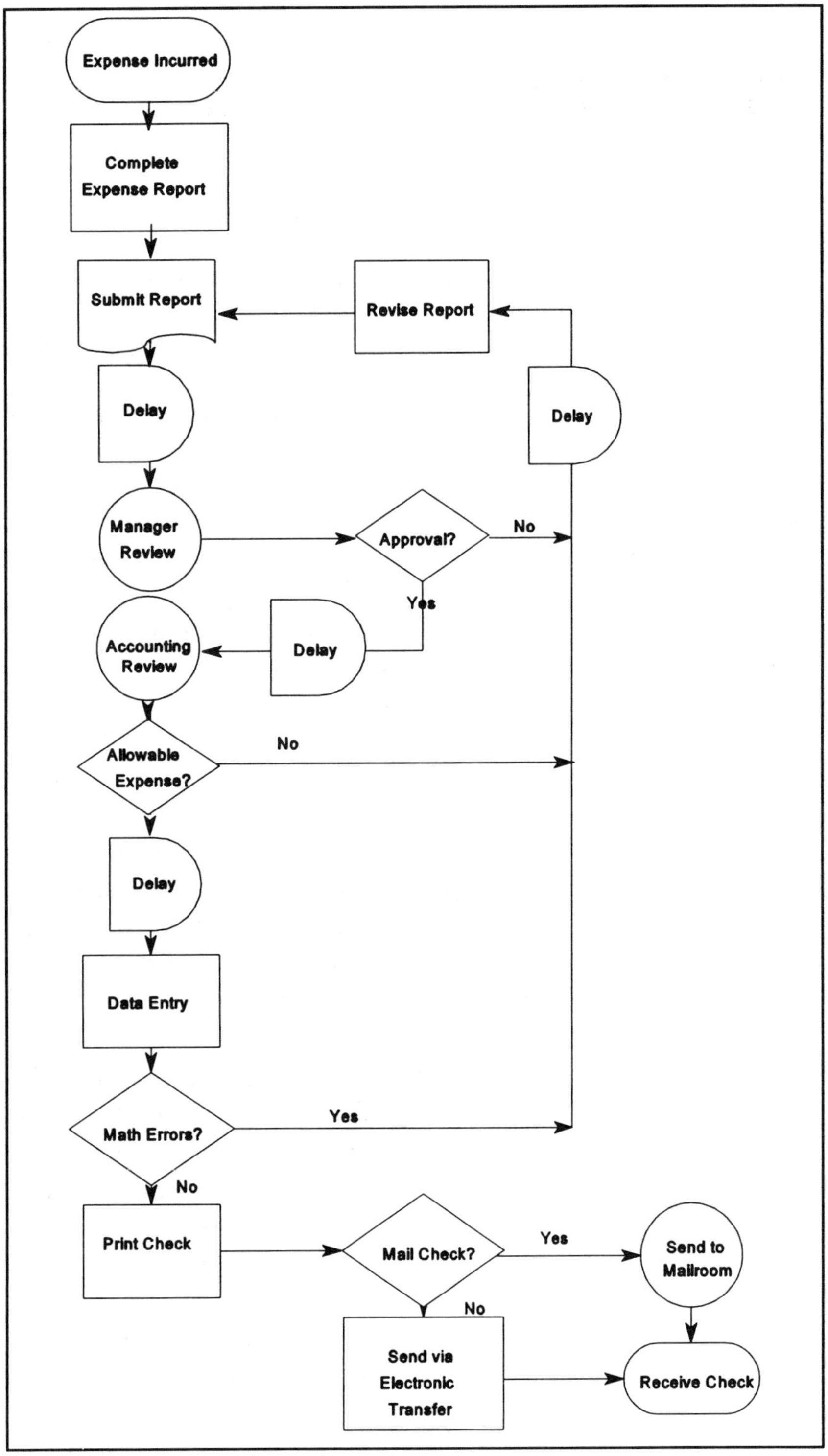

Figure 4-5

Tips

Guidelines for Developing Flowcharts:

✏ Be sure to consistently use the standard flowchart symbols.

✏ Make sure the chart reflects sufficient detail to identify value-added and nonvalue-added activities.

✏ Make sure every decision box has two clearly labeled exits.

✏ Use simple, concise activity descriptions.

✏ Define the beginning and end of the flowchart clearly.

✏ Be careful to identify all movements and delays.

Using Process Charts to Improve the Process

It will become apparent that simply documenting the current process via flowcharting will reveal improvement opportunities. Inevitably, a moderate degree of charting will prompt jarring questions such as, "Why do we do this step at all?" or "What if we could have the output without waiting?"

Once the charting of a process is complete, and prior to incorporating the tools explained later in this text, step back and make an objective evaluation of the process chart. It is likely that some surprisingly significant redesign can be accomplished rather quickly by looking for the following opportunities:

❶ Eliminate or minimize nonvalue-added steps
❷ Move inspection points forward
❸ Eliminate the need for inspection points altogether
❹ Evaluate inputs and suppliers
❺ Measure cycle time
❻ Combine operations or move steps into another process
❼ Eliminate operations or steps altogether
❽ Change the order of operations to make process simpler
❾ Automate or mechanize steps or operations
❿ Standardize operations

❶   Eliminate or minimize nonvalue-added steps

Generally, in analyzing process charts the objective is to identify and distinguish <u>value-added activities</u> from <u>nonvalue-added activities</u>. Value-added activities are the only activities that serve to create customer satisfaction and fulfill customer needs. The key to this technique is in having your customers' needs, wants, and expectations clearly defined, understood and documented.

- **Value-added activity** is a step, task or activity which contributes measurably to satisfying the customer, the user of the product or service.

- **Nonvalue-added activity** is a step, task or activity that the customer does not need and is not willing to pay for, or that does not fulfill a business requirement.

Movement and delay are always nonvalue-added activities. Four things happen when you move something, stop, then move it again:

①   Cycle time increases
②   Work in process increases
③   Costs go up
④   Errors are introduced

Inspection is also always a nonvalue-added activity. If proper planning and design of a process is made, inspection can be avoided by building in defect-free characteristics. Thus, inspection costs are minimized by eliminating errors or defects before they occur.

❷   Move inspection points forward

A key principle of quality improvement and process reengineering is to prevent errors and avoid rework loops. One way to move toward this goal is to place inspection (error catching) steps as close as possible to the point where the errors occur.

❸ **Eliminate the need for inspection points altogether**

If the point in the process where errors occur can be identified, it should be possible to eliminate these altogether. Chapters 7 and 8 provide tools for determining the root causes of process errors. Chapters 5 and 6 identify creative thinking and the customer orientation needed to create alternative processes.

❹ **Evaluate inputs and suppliers**

Whether your suppliers are internal or external to the organization, you are their customer and you should expect quality of their input, just as your customers expect quality output from you. To be a good customer to your suppliers, you should communicate to them what you want, need, and expect (i.e., your requirements). Additionally, it is generally more efficient and less costly to consolidate vendors and suppliers whenever possible. This has the effect of reducing the costs of processing accounts payable and inventory.

❺ **Measure cycle time**

Total cycle time is the time it takes to complete a process, from boundary to boundary.

Theoretical cycle time is the sum of the time required to perform each step in the process. This does not account for handoff or wait times and is theoretically the shortest time to complete the process.

The difference between total and theoretical cycle times represents an opportunity for improvement.

➏   **Combine operations or move steps into another process.**

It is often possible to combine operations or move one or more steps to an earlier point in the process as a means of reducing cycle time, making them part of a different, less time-sensitive process.

➐   **Eliminate activities or steps altogether.**

By eliminating, combining or streamlining steps within the process, theoretical cycle time can also be reduced.

➑   **Change the order of operations to make the process simpler.**

➒   **Automate or mechanize steps or operations (enhance technology).**

➓   **Standardize operations.**

Tips

✎   Often the first reaction to Process maps and charts is, "These are just flowcharts. We've always had these." Perhaps this is so, but traditional work flowcharts:

- Were done long ago when a process was first designed;

- Are done without input from those doing the work;

- Describe what someone <u>thinks</u> happens, not what <u>really</u> happens;

- Are not used to examine the requirements of both people and workflow; and

- Are not used to look for performance improvements and breakthroughs.

✏ Most teams inevitably step into the "should be" before analyzing the "as is." Individuals within a work group often discover that they do parts of the job differently from one another. How then, can the group accommodate and display these differences? The easy solution is to make premature decisions about what the one best way should be. We encourage you to separate the "as is" from the "should be" so that the development of improvements gains the careful, focused consideration it deserves.

✏ There are many computer based tools for process mapping and charting that can significantly increase the efficiency of these activities. Many of these tools include process measurement criteria and can be used to capture the improvement of processes in quantifiable terms (see also Chapter 9). Several packages include modeling techniques that can simulate several **"what if"** scenarios to determine impact on cycle time and process cost.

Exercise

Prepare a flow chart of the sequence of activities you follow to get to work each morning. Determine how this process might be improved to arrive at work earlier.

Functional Business Model

When initially defining your processes, a functional business model provides a simple way to organize the core business processes and subprocesses of the organization. It is simply an outline consisting of the major functional areas of a business.

To create a functional business model, list each major functional area of your department, unit, or business. Under each of the main functional areas list the major activities performed for each function. A third level can be utilized for a more detailed listing of functional business activities.

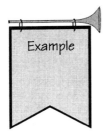

John Q. Public, CPA, is analyzing the way his public accounting firm performs services. With the help of his partners and staff, John developed the following functional business model:

1. Compliance services
    a. Attestation services
        1) Audit
        2) Compilation & Review
        3) Other
    b. Tax services
        1) Individual
        2) Corporate
        3) Partnership
        4) Estate
2. Advisory Services
    a. Financial
    b. Systems
    c. Tax

Furthermore, under each of the specific services, John and his team identified 3 subprocesses: 1-Gather information; 2-Analyze information; 3-Report on information.

Product Life Cycle

Any product or service has a life cycle. A life cycle begins at the earliest point the need for the product or service is identified. During the life of the product or service, inputs are consumed, outputs are created, and transformations of materials and information occur. The life cycle ends when all activity has been performed on the product or service.

A product life cycle analysis lists all of the activities in order of performance. A product or service may be defined as a subset of the entire process in order to break the analysis into "bite size" life cycles.

A product life cycle is a quick, easy and graphical method to gather information for additional modeling.

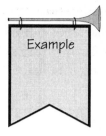

Example

Almost any activity can be viewed as a process beginning with an event which serves as the trigger. For example, mowing the lawn is a process that begins when we notice that the grass is long. The following is a life cycle analysis of mowing the lawn.

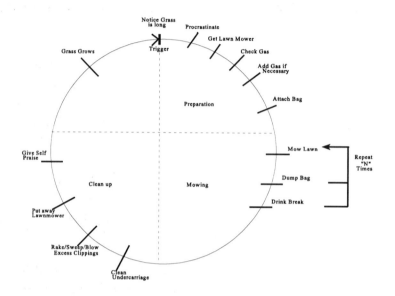

Figure 4-6

Information Usage Models

Information usage models (IUM) graphically depict the flow of data through a department or organization. In today's electronic office environment much of the information is generated and transmitted separately from the work product. Rather than focusing on the work activities in a process, IUMs are concerned with information flow.

As the use of local and wide area networks have proliferated the business world, the issues of information availability and access have become increasingly important. An IUM can be useful in capturing both the apparent and invisible transfer of data among processes.

Another key feature of the IUM is its ability to capture control points over the processing of data. There are checks on the integrity of data at various points in a process. These integrity checks may be performed through an inspection process or automatically by electronic equipment. These key control points often become the point at which a measurement is taken (see Chapter 9).

Components of an IUM

The general components of an IUM are as follows:

- Sources of data
- Users of data
- Information flows
- Processes
- Data stores
- Control points

Sources of data can be internal or external. Internal sources include departments, divisions or individuals within your organization. A process that is outside of the scope of your model can also be a source of data.

Users of data can also be internal or external to your company. The users are the customers of your process. Users generally require the information for some specific purpose.

Information flows depict the movement of information between sources and users of data, processes and data stores. Although IUMs are primarily concerned with information, products or services can also be considered information.

Processes have been defined extensively in Chapters 1 through 3 of this text. As in any analysis, the processes are the focus of the improvement effort.

Data stores are temporary or final resting places for the information. Data stores can be a computer file, filing cabinet, in-box or other holding area.

Control points are the integrity checks performed on the data. Control points may be an inspection of the data, observation of an activity or a duplication of an activity. The control point can be performed by an individual or automatically by a computer or some testing equipment.

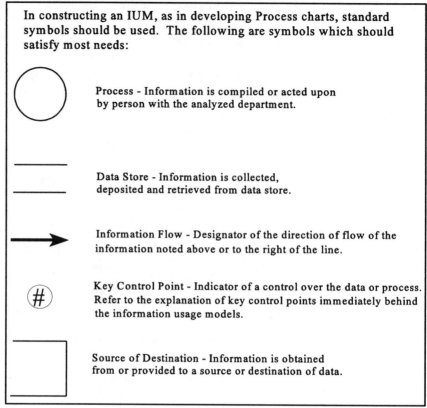

Figure 4-7

Constructing an IUM

❶   Identify the processes and/or subprocesses
❷   Identify the major functions performed in the
     processes
❸   Identify the sources and users of data
❹   Identify the flows of data between sources of data,
     processes and users of data
❺   Identify the data stores and their contents
❻   Identify control points

❶   **Identify the processes and/or subprocesses**

The process is the central focus of the analysis effort in a
process improvement program. The processes or
subprocesses used in the IUM will determine the level of
detail of the IUM. The more detailed the process, the more
detailed the information should be that you gather
regarding the information flow.

Processes are depicted by circles in the center portion of the page. Each circle should represent the same level of process from your functional business model or process maps.

❷ **Identify the major functions performed in the processes**

The identification of major functions is required to get the detailed level regarding information flows. Major functions are not depicted on the IUM.

❸ **Identify the sources and users of data**

Sources of data are the suppliers of information for the process. Internal sources of information can be other departments, business units or processes. Internal sources of data are represented by a rectangle with an open left side.

An external source of data could be a customer, supplier, or an information company such as a credit bureau. The symbol for an external source is the same as that for an internal source with an extra line inside of the right side of the rectangle (see Figure 4-8).

Sources of data are drawn on the left side of the page. Distinction between internal and external sources is primarily for use later in the project when the team attempts to change the data flows.

Internal and external users of data may come from the same groups as that for sources of data. The symbol for data users is the same as that for sources with the open side of the rectangle on the right. The symbols for uses of data are placed on the right side of the page.

The order of the sources and users on the page is not important. Place the sources symbols close to the process that it supplies.

Computers or other data stores are *never* sources or users of data. Data stores must be acted upon by a process to be a source of data.

❹   **Identify the flows of data between sources of data, processes and users of data**

Information consists of reports, invoices or other paperwork, E-mail, rumor mills, etc. Information flows can be in one direction or bi-directional.

Information flows are indicated with arrows from a source, data store, or process to a source, process, data store, or user. Above each data line is a description of the data. A bidirectional line is appropriate only if the data is unchanged at the process and the data is physically moved.

❺   **Identify the data stores and their contents**

The most common data store is a computer. Data stores are indicated by two parallel lines above and below the description of the data store. The level of detail used in the IUM should relate to the detail level of the processes modeled. A detailed model may indicate data stores using a data library. A macro model may use a designation such as PC Lan or AS 400 Mainframe.

❻   **Identify control points**

Control points are checks on the system that ensure compliance with procedures or intended results. Controls are of a preventative or inspective nature. Chapter 9 includes a detailed discussion of controls and their related cost. Identification of controls allow for later analysis of the cost/benefit relation of those controls.

Control points are designated by numbered arrows. The description of the controls are generally too detailed to be included on the page. The IUM is generally supplemented by a controls listing that describes the nature and purpose of each numbered control point.

The diagram flows on the page from left to right. Similar to a process model depicted in Figure 4-3, an information model begins with inputs, which are transformed by a process containing activities, resulting in outputs.

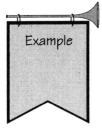

Example

The following IUM is based upon the professional society text and reference book Life Cycle Analysis.

Text and Reference Books

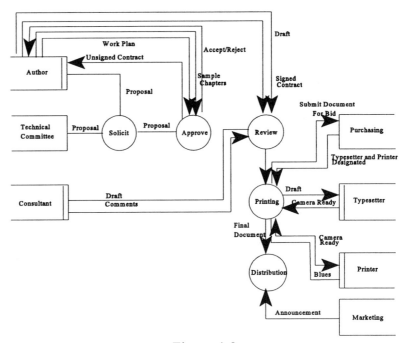

Figure 4-8

Tips

✏   Functional business model, product life cycle, and process maps are useful tools for determining the level of detail required for a useful IUM. If your model begins with processes that are too broad, the number of information flows identified will be too large for easy analysis.

✏   One practical way to identify the data flow is to start at the beginning of a process and track the information through the activities identified in step three. Brainstorm for additional sources of information with people close to the process.

Teamwork - People and Creativity Skills

Chapter Objectives

Effective Process Management results from teams formed to improve, redesign and manage a business process. Whether the teams are functional, cross functional, networked, or supervisory in nature, people and creativity skills are essential for maximum effectiveness.

In order for a work team or project team to succeed in its task, it needs more than technical knowledge of the area under investigation. While expertise in the subject at hand is vital, participants in a successful project must also understand how to:

- work together as a team
- conduct productive meetings
- resolve conflicts
- gather and analyze data
- communicate results
- implement changes

This chapter provides an understanding of the principles and techniques related to:

☞   Team characteristics
☞   Team building
☞   Team behavior tools
☞   Conflict resolution tools
☞   Meeting management tools

Team Characteristics

A **team** is a group of people working *inter*dependently toward a common *goal*. Teams are not a new concept. Every business is comprised of a series of teams set up to solve problems or pursue objectives. The predominant team structure in a "typical" business is that of **functional teams** organized into departments. A functional team is a group of individuals who have similar skills that enable them to perform a particular task. A finance department comprised of analysts is an example of a functional team.

In a redesign effort, **cross-functional teams** are more prevalent. A cross-functional team is a group of individuals with different, and hopefully complimentary, skills that combine to achieve a goal or function. A football team is a good example of a cross-functional team. The offense and defense are comprised of skilled individuals who perform different functions with the common goal of winning a game.

When Teams are Appropriate

Teams are not required for **all** redesign activities. The use of teams is appropriate for projects that require:

- A high level of **creativity**
- Crossing **organizational boundaries**
- **Commitment** to be successful
- **Diverse expertise**

Creativity is the ability or power to create original and expressive ideas. Every individual has a degree of creativity. A team environment can bring out the creativity of individuals and combine the creativity of team members to form imaginative ideas.

When a project crosses **organizational boundaries**, cross functional teams are required to ensure that the activities of the project positively influence all affected departments.

Commitment is the state of being bound emotionally or intellectually to a course of action or to another person or persons. Commitment is a deeper characteristic than acceptance. People may accept a decision without being committed to it.

Diverse expertise refers to the broad base of knowledge required to solve complex problems. Creativity and commitment may not be enough to determine the most efficient process that crosses departmental boundaries.

Figure 5-1 plots the type of decision required based upon the commitment required of personnel who will be bound by the decision, versus the accuracy required in the decision-making process.

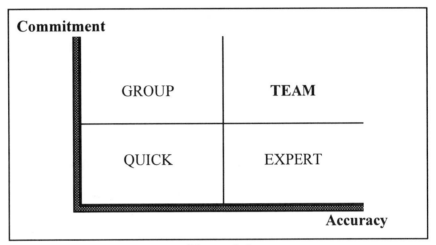

Figure 5-1

Quick decisions do not require much buy-in or accuracy. For example, if your building is on fire, no meetings will be required to gain a consensus that leaving the building is appropriate. Neither does it require an advanced college degree to determine what to do.

Expert decisions require the knowledge of a specialist but not the commitment from the organization. For example, when determining what cable will be run for a computer network, most network users will not care to be involved in the decision process. What is required is an expert who understands the hardware requirements.

Group decisions may not require a great deal of expertise, but they do require acceptance from those who are expected to comply with the decision. For example, when planning a relocation, determining where individuals will be placed in the new office does not require the level of expertise needed to choose the new location. However, if people are indiscriminately placed in the new location without regard for working and interpersonal relationships, productivity may suffer.

Team decisions are appropriate when both buy-in *and* expertise are required. Teams use a consensus style of decision-making.

Team Charter

Every team formed should develop a team charter. The charter focuses the action of a team and usually includes:

❶ Team mission statement
❷ Quantitative and qualitative goals
❸ Projected team impact
❹ Listing of team members
❺ Guidelines for attainment of goals

❶ Team Mission Statement

Just as the organization as an entity should have a mission statement, so should each team. A mission statement provides the focal point for the team's existence. It should include who the team is, what it is formed to do, and for whom and why it is functioning. A good mission statement is short, inspiring and easy to remember.

❷ Quantitative and Qualitative Goals

Goal setting is one of the most important activities for effective teams. Although goals may be partially or wholly determined by upper management, they should be agreed upon or modified by the team. The best method for setting goals is by the team itself with acceptance by upper management.

The goals should be directed towards meeting the needs of the teams and the customer. As such, objectives should be worded in language familiar to the customer. Goals should be attainable, but challenging in order to bring out the best in the team.

The goals should be both quantitative and qualitative.

Quantitative goals may include reduction in cost by a specified percentage or improvement in customer satisfaction by a factor. Numeric goals should be measurable and objectively determinable.

Other goals can be qualitative, such as improving the perception or presentation of a product, process or service. Although qualitative goals may not be as easily measured, they can be specific enough for a subjective determination of achievement.

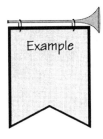

Example

The marketing department of XYZ Company keeps a file of all client correspondence. Once a client is obtained, the customer service department uses the file to maintain a record of all customer correspondence, including complaints and service requests. As information is received, it is placed on top of the file.

XYZ organized a team of salespeople, service technicians and customer service representatives with the goal of improving the usability of the customer correspondence file.

The team developed a standard file format with tabbed dividers and a standardized filing procedure. The new file and system have increased technician and customer service representative satisfaction.

❸ **Projected Team Impact**

The process of redesign will affect more than just the team members. Other business processes that supply information or materials to the process as well as customers of the process will be affected by the redesign effort. Although the changes will hopefully be positive in nature, all processes and individuals that might be impacted by the redesign should be informed and included in the redesign effort.

The team charter should include a listing of impacted processes. The stakeholders and/or process owners of those processes should be informed of the projected effect of the redesign. The team should include members of those processes identified.

❹   **Listing of Team Members**

Members of a team are selected for their expertise in the process or the skills they possess. It is important for all team members to know the relative strengths and weaknesses of the team and its members. A listing of technical and people skills required by the team is an initial step in this direction.

One tool commonly used to examine the environment facing a team is called **S**trengths, **W**eaknesses, and future **O**pportunities and **T**hreats **(S.W.O.T.)** analysis. This identification exercise helps team members develop an understanding of the team's situation and compare assumptions about the team and its members. The results can be mapped on a chart similar to Figure 5-2 to graphically view the relationships.

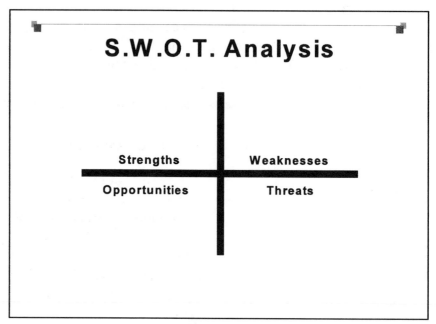

Figure 5-2

S.W.O.T. analysis is also commonly used for strategic planning.

❺   **Guidelines for Attainment of Goals**

Teams will be held responsible and accountable for their
actions. Teams typically operate with limited resources and
have constraints on their time allocated to a project. These
limitations will affect the attainment of goals and should be
considered when establishing goals. By clearly stating
resources and time available for the project in the charter,
all parties will understand the guidelines under which the
team is operating.

Team Roles and Responsibilities

Redesign teams are usually formed to solve some existing problem
or take advantage of an identified opportunity. To ensure that the
team meets its goals, the team must be composed of the right
individuals. Sometimes the team members and their roles are
defined by management. Allowing senior management to decide
who the team members are, and what their roles should be, usually
ensures that the skills and expertise required for the project are
dedicated.

At other times members and their roles are determined by a team or
through volunteer recruiting. Allowing the staff to make these
decisions will increase the ownership in the project, but may result
in underfunding of the project or a team with missing skill sets.

A combination of the two approaches may be most appropriate
depending upon the corporate culture and stage of the overall
reengineering effort. Additionally, team members may have
different responsibilities during the life of a team. To avoid
misunderstandings, it is important for all team members to know
one another's roles and responsibilities.

Typical redesign team members are:

❶   Team Leader
❷   Process Owner
❸   Facilitator
❹   Team Member

❶ **Team Leader**

Quite often a team leader is chosen in advance by upper management. When chosen by management, this person is often the process owner, department head or other position with authority. However, a person with authoritative or bureaucratic clout is not always best suited for the role of team leader. As discussed in various sections of this chapter, the role of a team leader is different than that of a department head.

The team leader is responsible for:

- **Providing direction** to the group
- The **content** of team activities
- Fulfilling the role of **project manager**

During problem solving sessions, the leader does not automatically take a "leadership" role. Other team members should be encouraged to assume that role. In fact, all members should practice it in order to understand the complexities of leadership and to gain the experience needed to be the leader of other teams.

Some individuals through their charisma or other personality traits are **natural influencers** and become informal leaders. These informal leaders are often turned to for advice, opinions and assistance.

❷ **Process Owner**

The process owner is an individual who has oversight responsibility for the process being studied. He or she may be the department head, manager, or foreman. The process owner should always be involved in final decisions affecting their process. The owner's level of knowledge of the mechanics and "big picture view" of the process is usually greater than that of other team members. As such, the owner will generally have insight as to how the effects of a change will ripple through the process.

The responsibility that the process owner maintains in the day-to-day operations of the process should not influence the operation of the group itself. There may be times when it is more appropriate for the owner to be absent from team meetings to ensure honest, open debate of the issues at stake.

❸ **Facilitator**

Facilitation is the **art** of leading groups to consensus by using the tools, techniques and processes that tap the collective genius of the group. The facilitator need not be an expert, and should not **tell** the team what to do. A facilitator:

- Guides, without directing
- Helps people self-discover new approaches and solutions to problems
- Harnesses disagreement into a source of alternatives, creativity and synergy

The facilitator is responsible for the team **decision making process** and for providing the group with the technical tools and techniques used in quality improvement. The facilitator is often a reengineering champion as described in Chapter 2.

As the team matures, the facilitator transfers knowledge to the members so they can assume responsibility for the duties a facilitator is initially required to perform.

❹ **Team Members**

The role of team member should not be overlooked. It should be obvious that each member has a responsibility to assume different roles at various times. Each member is expected to actively share their expertise and opinion and should work to make the team cohesive.

Selecting team members is crucial to the initial effectiveness and the ability to guide the team to peak performance. Teams should be limited to 8-12 individuals depending upon the size of the company and project. Although encouraging participation at all levels of the organizational structure is valuable, the compatibility of team members is critical.

The size of these teams usually allows for representation of all stakeholders in the process, including people from various functional levels as well as required specialists. Large teams tend to lose the decisiveness and consensus building dynamics available in smaller teams.

Team Building

Teams are formed in various ways and for different purposes. Depending upon how and why a team is formed will influence its structure and performance. A team formed through a mandate will experience more difficulty becoming a cohesive unit than a group that formed by itself to solve a particular problem.

Although it seems unlikely that teams may form without a direct mandate from management, in quality driven organizations it is a common occurrence. Regardless of how they are formed, teams follow a logical progression of growth. This progression is referred to as a **team model**.

A team model provides a pattern for evaluating the growth of a team. There are a number of models depicting the evolution of a team over time. One common model is Tuckman's Model which outlines the stages of team growth as:

- **Forming**, during which the team is formed and becomes acquainted;
- **Storming**, during which the "pecking" or structure of the team order is established;
- **Norming**, during which conflicts arising during the storming stage are resolved and the norms that will guide the behaviors within the group are established; and
- **Performing**, during which the group accomplishes its best work.

Until a team reaches the performing stage, the team has not reached peak efficiency. Characteristics of effective teams include:

- **Respect** - People can speak their mind and air their differences without fear of retribution or ridicule. Any member can point out when the conversation is "off topic" but also allows others to speak even when the opinion differs from their own.
- **Mutual Support** - Competition between team members is non-existent. When a team member requests help it can be provided without fear of hidden agendas. As such, the skills and competencies of individual team members can be applied where most useful.
- **Conflict Resolution** - Conflicts will exist even in performing groups. Effective teams will recognize the conflicts and work through them to reach a consensus or minimize the effects of the disagreement.

Cohesiveness

Cohesiveness is sometimes described as the team's attraction or affinity for itself and its members. Generally speaking, cohesive work groups act differently due to the following factors:

- **Informational Influence** - Without information to the contrary, we tend to believe groups we associate with.
- **Normative Influence** - A desire to belong to a team will influence the individual members to work up to the standards of the group.
- **Conflict Resolution** - Differences between members will be disturbing to other members of the group. Members will usually attempt to resolve these conflicts.

A team which has evolved to the norming or performing stage will be more cohesive than teams in the earlier stages of maturity. There are a variety of tools that can accelerate a group's progression through the various stages in the model. These tools can be loosely grouped into **team behavior, conflict resolution, and meeting management tools.**

Team Behavior Tools

Included in the array of team behavior tools are a variety of techniques to improve the creativity and efficiency of teams. Creativity is a state of mind. It is not something you have or do not have, but something that can be nurtured and developed.

Conventional problem solving techniques are analytical in nature. Considering the possible solutions, alternatives are analyzed to determine the most feasible or best solution.

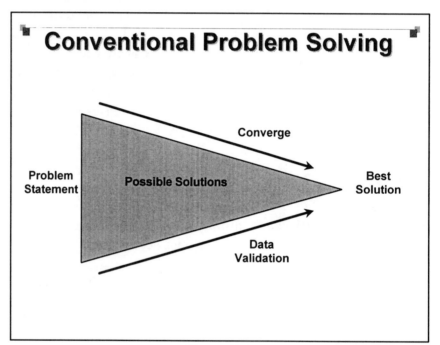

Figure 5-3

Creative problem solving begins with the same problem statement, but focuses on the generation of all possible solutions. The goal is to expand your mental capacity to consider a broad range of alternatives.

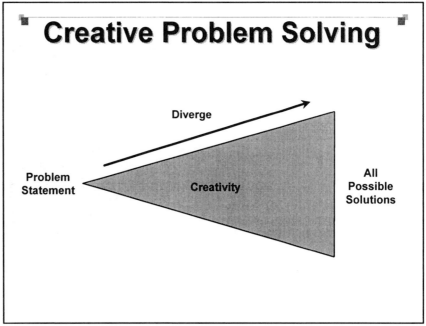

Figure 5-4

Productive thinking is the combination of conventional and creative thinking. By beginning with creative thinking, more alternatives including new, creative solutions will be developed. Once the range of solutions has been expanded, analytical tools can be used to determine the most feasible solution.

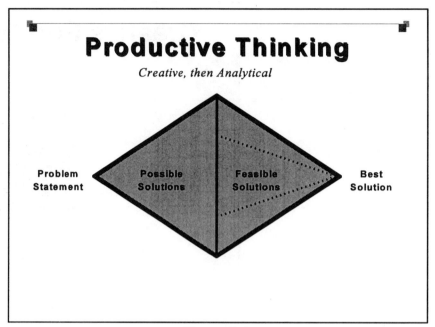

Figure 5-5

The advantage of team decision-making is the ability of teams to generate more possible and feasible solutions than an individual.

Brainstorming

One of the best known and most useful creativity tools is brainstorming. Brainstorming is a technique which encourages the generation of a large number of ideas, in a short time, from a group.

Steps in Brainstorming:

❶ State the problem or topic.
❷ Generate ideas following brainstorming guidelines.
❸ Allow time for thoughts to incubate and seek outside input.
❹ Resume brainstorming.
❺ Clarify and evaluate ideas.

Brainstorming Guidelines:

- Record all ideas.
- Ensure that all team members participate. Consider participating in sequence around the room, one idea per turn.
- Do not allow criticism, comments, or evaluation while generating ideas.
- Purposefully "free-wheel" and encourage "piggy-backing" on other ideas.
- Strive for quantity.

List Reduction

List reduction involves processing the output of a brainstorming session. The objective of list reduction is to clarify the options so that all team members understand them, then reducing the options to a manageable number. List reduction can involve asking for more information, clarifying statements, and combining similar ideas into a single statement.

Brainwriting

Brainwriting is a technique similar to brainstorming. To allow for anonymous submission of ideas, pass out index cards for recording of ideas. Each team member may submit as many ideas as they like, one idea per card. The cards can then be gathered and redistributed to other team members who add additional suggestions or ideas to make the thought more workable.

Tips

☞   List reduction can be the painful part of the productive thinking process. It is easy to brainstorm and list ideas, especially when you know there will not be any criticism of your ideas. When reducing the list to a manageable size, eliminate ideas, utilizing criteria which has been agreed upon.

Begin your list reduction with a gross filter to weed out obviously inappropriate suggestions. This filter may be the application of the team mission statement. If the suggestion does not contribute to the mission, it is eliminated. Then review the list using tighter criteria until a manageable number of ideas remains.

✏ Brainwriting, as opposed to brainstorming, may be more appropriate when the presence of one or more individuals may influence the free exchange of ideas. When a superior is present some team members may be intimidated and inhibited. The inhibited individual may not present their ideas for fear of repercussion or ridicule. Brainwriting allows a degree of anonymity which may enable the person to overcome the inhibitions.

Nominal Group Technique

Nominal group technique provides a way for all team members to have an equal voice in problem selection.

Steps in Nominal Group Technique

❶ Everyone in the group writes a problem they feel is most important on a slip of paper.

❷ These slips are collected and the problem statements are written on a flip chart or white board.

❸ Duplications are removed and problem statements are clarified if necessary.

❹ Each problem statement is designated with a letter (A,B,C,D,etc.). The number of letters is added up.

❺ Each individual ranks all problems in descending order. If there were five problem statements each statement would be ranked in order of importance 5,4,3,2,1, with 5 being the most important.

❻ The scores are totaled.

The problem with the highest total score would be deemed most important to the group as a whole.

Delphi Exchange

A similar creativity tool to Brainwriting and Nominal Group Technique is known as a Delphi Exchange. Each team or sub-group of a team develops a proposal or chart of ideas. The ideas are then exchanged among groups for written comments and returned to the originating group.

Context Mapping

Context maps are graphical representations of thought processes. When we think analytically it is said that we are using our left brain, concentrating on logic and words. When we think creatively it is said that we are using our right brain, focusing on colors, shapes and patterns. Context maps foster creativity and innovation in thinking by using a "whole brain" approach. In a context map, information is organized by association rather than in orderly categories.

Mindmapping

Mindmapping is the most widely recognized form of context mapping. By organizing information through association, mindmapping can enhance creativity and identify characteristics, attributes and qualities often taken for granted.

Steps in Mindmapping

❶ Reduce a problem, issue, or theme to a single word or short phrase.

❷ Draw association branches from the central statement.

❸ Secondary associations are drawn as limbs to the branch.

❹ Keep drawing branches, secondary branches, even twigs, until you run out of ideas.

When adding branches to the central statement, primary branches or secondary branches, allow the association to occur freely without evaluating them as you draw.

Evaluation of the location of branches can be performed immediately after you finish the map, or at a subsequent meeting after the map has been "fully digested" by the team members. Interrelationships between the branches can be connected by a different color pen or marker.

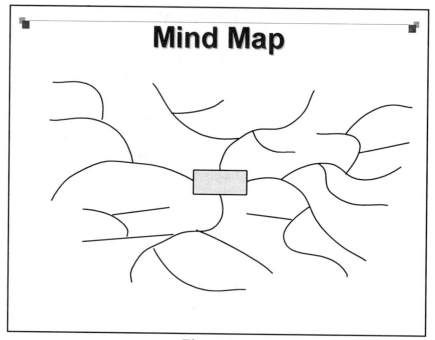

Figure 5-6

Tips

✏   Mindmapping has been found to be extremely applicable in focus group research on the topic of quality. As definitions of attributes associated with quality are often taken for granted, mindmaps are a good tool to draw out these difficult to recognize factors.

Conflict Resolution Tools

The advantage of teams is the ability to combine the thoughts, talents and experience of individuals. This advantage can only be realized when the team members agree and support the decisions of the group.

Conflict resolution tools are used to avoid counterproductive situations such as extended conflicts and emotional attachments to group decisions. When properly managed, conflict can be positive, enhancing the team's ability to see "outside the box" of conventional thought.

Consensus

Consensus can be defined as the collective opinion of a group, which is reached by:

- **Listening** to all sides;
- **Agreeing** to a decision-making process; and
- **Supporting** the results of that process.

Consensus is commonly understood to mean unanimous agreement, but in team situations it is usually defined as acceptance and willingness to support the group decision.

To determine whether the team has reached a consensus, the facilitator or discussion leader may ask the following three questions:

❶   *Does everyone accept the decision?*
An affirmative answer denotes a decision has been made.

❷   *Is there any opposition to this decision?*
No response generally denotes acceptance. Non-verbal indications of opposition should be noted and explored.

❸   *Can everyone live with this decision?*
A "yes" ensures that no one has any conflicts with the decision.

As depicted in Figure 5-7, as the size of the team increases, the time required to reach consensus increases geometrically.

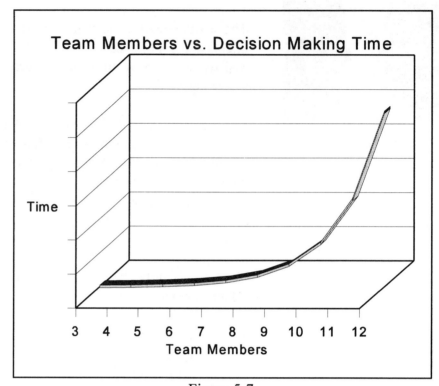

Team Members vs. Decision Making Time

Figure 5-7

Team Profiles Matrix

During team formation, or when new members join a team, a thorough introduction of individuals is important. Team members should introduce themselves, give a summary of their work background, interests, a statement of their expectations regarding the project, and "hot buttons" for which they have great conviction. This profile can be captured for all team members and circulated.

Excerpts from the profiles can be included in the team charter. These profiles can be useful in determining and understanding the frictions that may occur between team members in later stages of team development.

Team Ground Rules

When a team forms, it should develop a list of group agreements that reflect expected behaviors of the members. These agreements, or ground rules, can be used to point out and correct problem behaviors.

Examples of team ground rules include:

- Meetings will start and end on time
- Everyone participates
- One person speaks at a time
- Ideas become group property

Every ground rule has a purpose. For example, people with time constraints want to know that their time will be used judiciously. Ideas become group property so an individual does not have the need to defend "their" idea. Therefore, discussion or dissent regarding an idea is not perceived as (or is) an attack on the individual who proposed the idea.

These ground rules can then be used to eliminate problem behaviors. A team member can politely refer to a ground rule when it is broken. Continuous or chronic violations can result in sanctioning by the team.

BATNA

Best Alternative To Negotiated Agreement (**BATNA**) is used to provide a standard against which to measure proposed agreements. Simply stated, before entering any negotiation, determine the conditions that must be met before accepting an agreement. These conditions should be based upon objective criteria and represent the interests of all parties.

Paint Two Positives

We are frequently faced with situations which cause an immediate negative reaction. When this happens, it is possible to force a positive examination of the issue. Create at least two positive reactions to the situation or problem. With practice, this technique can result in the examination of seemingly negative issues for positive elements.

Yes; and ...

"Yes; and..." is used to build on existing or proposed ideas in a positive way. A team member will start each sentence with the words "yes; and..." In this manner, the member is accepting whatever the previous member said and building upon it.

This technique can be used for creating group synergy in Brainstorming by having one person propose a step and another person saying, "yes; and..." adding something to the first proposal. The goal is to stop evaluative thinking which slows the flow of creative ideas.

Thermometer

A thermometer analogy is used to display team members' subjective assessments of one or more intangibles. Draw a thermometer and, in place of degrees, list some other scale of indicators. For example, Figure 5-8 shows a thermometer used to track team attitude. In this case, the scale runs from "lousy" at the bottom through "poor, fair, acceptable, good, great, outstanding and incredible."

One strategy is to pass out copies of the thermometer and allow team members to anonymously mark them. The team leader can then report on the distribution of the scores.

Process Redesign & Management: Beyond Reengineering
© 1995 Windham Brannon Business Advisory Services, LLC

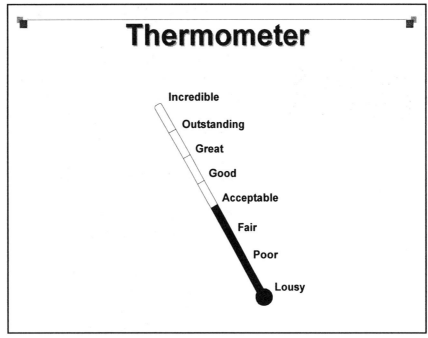

Figure 5-8

Balance Sheets

In contrast to context diagrams, balance sheets (also known as T accounts) place ideas into pro and con categories. By placing choices into these categories, teams can document alternatives and move a group closer to consensus.

To create a balance sheet, set up a large grid with two columns and a row for each of the options. Label the columns "+" and "-", then enter the positive and negative aspects of each option in turn.

Balance sheets are quick and easy to use but are not intended as a decision-making tool. They organize information to facilitate discussion among team members in an effort to reach a consensus. A decision-making tool that is similar in appearance is called Force Field Analysis (see Chapter 7).

Tips

✐   Balance sheets are especially useful when evaluating the positive and negative comments about the meeting process itself.

Meeting Management Tools

The team meeting is the focal point for the activities of the group. The more effective the team meetings are, the more effective the group becomes. During the meeting, decisions are made, responsibilities are assigned, action plans are created, and performance is gauged.

Roles and Responsibilities

To facilitate effective group interaction and decision-making, team members should assume the following roles:

> ❶   Discussion leader
> ❷   Facilitator
> ❸   Scribe
> ❹   Timekeeper

❶   Discussion Leader

The discussion leader is the individual who is responsible for the overall management of the particular meeting, and may or may not be the group leader. Group leaders often abdicate the meeting leadership responsibilities to team members.

The discussion leader's responsibilities include:

- Establishing and communicating the agenda prior to the meeting;
- Setting up the meeting facilities, including arranging for adequate space, supplies and equipment;
- Managing the meeting, including introduction of topics to be discussed and ensuring participation of all members.

The importance of an **effective agenda** should not be overlooked. Advance circulation of agendas allow group members to prepare for meetings and ensure that all necessary items are addressed. In addition to topics for discussion and allocated time, agendas should state the purpose of the meeting and materials that should be reviewed prior to and/or required at the meeting.

The meeting facilities can greatly affect the productivity and efficiency of the meeting. If the facilities are too small or hot, participants will be uncomfortable and unproductive. The seating arrangements should be comfortable and allow all members clear sight of one another as well as flip charts or wall screens. All necessary equipment should be on hand so that valuable time is not wasted searching for supplies.

During the meeting, the discussion leader should take a seat that is not associated with power or authority. The leader is an equal member, not a superior. When it is time to guide the discussion forward, or time allotted for discussion has expired, the leader can assert himself. Sometimes a separate role of **policeman** or **sergeant** is created to ensure that discussion does not get off-track or that time constraints are enforced.

❷ **Facilitator**

The facilitator's role is to free the group from internal obstacles or difficulties so that it may efficiently and effectively pursue its objective(s). This role is often performed by a person who is not a regular member of the group such as an outside consultant. Other times the role is performed by a reengineering champion or a company facilitator. Regardless of who has the formal responsibility for facilitating the meeting, all team members must share in the responsibility for making a session as effective as possible.

❸ **Scribe**

An often overlooked role in a team meeting is that of scribe. The scribe records the activities of the group such as agenda minutes, goals, decisions, action items, agreements, disagreements, plans, brainstormed lists, etc.

The scribe must record the information intelligibly, though not necessarily neatly or graphically. However, many of the quality tools are graphical and pictures are often more stimulating than words. What is important is that everyone's idea(s) are captured exactly and in context. It is not necessary to capture every word verbatim like a stenographer, but to record information that is agreeable to those asking it to be transcribed.

Periodically the scribe should review the notes with comments such as:

> "I've put down ...", or
> "Does this fairly state what you were saying?"

Recording information on flip charts, using size and color to denote emphasis, importance or differences, is useful for capturing the essence of the meeting.

After the meeting is completed, minutes and other documentation should be forwarded to participants. This information can be reviewed and agreed upon at the subsequent meeting.

❹ **Timekeeper**

In most team situations, groups have time constraints. Problem solving and employee involvement groups generally have meetings that last one to two hours. Although they may have more flexibility, redesign work groups also have constraints.

To manage their time effectively, most groups will agree on time allotted to each agenda item as the first order of business. The timekeeper is assigned the responsibility for:

- Leading the initial discussion allocating time to the tasks;
- Monitoring how long the group is taking to accomplish its tasks; and
- Giving regular updates to make group members aware of the status of the meeting or the item at hand.

It is common for a group to reallocate its time as the meeting progresses. The team may decide not to complete the task within the time limit, to extend the time limit, or to table a topic completely. These are group decisions and are *not* the timekeeper's individual choice.

Tips

✐ There are many software packages available for managing meeting activities. Some packages are fully integrated to encompass the entire meeting process, from meeting announcement to recording the meeting effectiveness.

✐ Fortunately for scribes who are not artistic, there are many technological advances to help graphically record meeting activities. Software packages can draw mind maps, process charts and a myriad of other graphical tools.

✐ Many teams enjoy using white boards rather than flip charts. White boards allow for erasing and changing of drawings and text as information is clarified. The downside to white boards is that someone, usually the scribe, has to transfer the information onto paper or computer. Some companies with extensive training facilities now have white boards with photocopying ability.

CAIRO

At different times during the life of a team, members will have varying levels of responsibility. Due to other work commitments, members may not be available at all times. At other times, the team may be tackling an area outside of a member's area of expertise. **CAIRO** is a simple pneumonic device to help recall the typical level of involvement of individuals. The letters stand for:

C - Consult
A - Advise
I - Involved
R - Responsible
O - Omitted, No involvement

This scheme can be used to define the responsibilities of team members for a specific task.

Communication

Communication is the process of one person sending information and another person receiving the information. The message is not always received as sent due to various filters and noise in the transmission.

Filters include personality and learning styles. Some people may be introverted while others are extroverted. Some people learn through reading and/or listening, while some require hands-on activities. In team settings, it is important to understand personality and learning styles of fellow members in order to send information that will penetrate their filters.

Sending - Speaking   **Filter - Noise**   **Receiving - Listening**

Active Listening

Another important aspect of communication is listening. Most of our formal communication training is centered around the transmission of data. We learn effective business writing and public speaking but are not formally instructed in **active listening**.

Active listening is a technique to improve communication between two individuals. It requires the listener to be an active participant in the communication process. Active participants take the speakers frame of reference and emotions into consideration while listening. They periodically check with the speaker to ensure that they are understanding what is said. Active listeners pay attention to body language, both their's and the speaker's.

Some basic active listening techniques are:

- **Mirroring** - Repeating back exactly what was said by the speaker;
- **Paraphrasing** - Rephrasing what was said in your own words;
- **Summary Statements** - Similar to a paraphrasing, summarily restate the core themes and feelings of the conversation, without evaluation, at the end of a long discussion;
- **Open-Ended Questioning** - Encourage the other person to talk at length by asking questions that cannot be answered with a simple yes or no;
- **Sensitivity to Body Language** - Clenched fists (anger), crossed arms (resistance or distance), and drumming fingers (impatience) are messages that must be heard;
- **Verbal Acknowledgment** - Simple sounds such as "uh-huh," "yes," or "OK" all convey that you are listening; and
- **Undivided Attention** - Move in front of your desk while the other person is talking, maintain eye contact, do not accept phone calls or interruptions, notice the speaker's humor.

Outcome

Discerning managers recognize that the results of using teams are dependent upon the individuals and their ability to work together. By furnishing structure, tools and techniques that encourage creativity management, project success can be enhanced.

By understanding the dynamics of teams and the individuals on their team, members can magnify their contributions. Listening and understanding the views of their teammates will broaden horizons and improve communication skills.

CHAPTER 6

Customer Orientation

Chapter Objectives

A customer orientation is based upon keeping customers satisfied so that they will want to do business with your organization. It is widely believed that customer retention significantly increases profitability. Customer orientation also improves the company's probability of attracting new customers.

> "Quality is judged by customers. All product and service characteristics that contribute value to the customer and lead to customer satisfaction and preference must be the focus of a company's management system."
>
> Malcolm Baldrige National Quality
> Award Core Values and Concepts
> *1994 Malcolm Baldrige Award Criteria*

This chapter identifies and demonstrates the tools used to identify and convert customer requirements into plans and actions. Specific contents of the chapter include:

- ☞ Voice of the customer analysis
- ☞ Service quality
- ☞ Quality function deployment

Concepts

Customer satisfaction can be defined as the extent a company:

- Meets the needs of the customer; and
- Provides value to the customer.

A customer can be considered *satisfied* if they will continue doing business with the company. A customer can be considered *delighted* if they will recommend the company to others.

Customer orientation is required throughout **all** processes at **all** times. Although this may sound extreme, customer orientation is one of the key concepts and building blocks of any quality system.

Any process not tied to customer satisfaction will create mixed messages to the employees and customers. For example:

- Compensation systems linked to production or volume will cause the employee to attempt to manipulate the production system to their personal benefit. If compensation is linked to customer values or satisfaction, the customer's best interest is in that employee's best interest.
- Purchasing activities based upon price considerations may not take fitness for use by the customer into consideration.

Example of mixed messages and misguided orientation

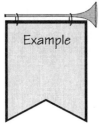

Example

Company X has announced that its policy is to sell the product that best fits the usage requirements of the customer.

- Company X offers a whole line of products that are similar in nature but are intended for somewhat strenuous operating conditions.
- Company X believes that it will retain customer satisfaction and loyalty by selling the appropriate product, resulting in greater long-term profits.
- The mid-line product has a cost that is 20% lower than the heavy duty product.
- Salesperson G receives commission based upon volume and profit margin. There is a greater profit margin on the high-end products.
- Customer A has been using a heavy duty product previously but would be equally well-served by a mid-line use product.
- If Customer A purchases one unit per month regardless of the product's durability, which product will Salesperson G sell?
- Which one would you sell?

Chapter 3 introduced the concept of identifying customers. The remainder of this chapter discusses how to identify customer needs and relate those needs to product, service and process quality.

Service Quality

Service quality refers to meeting the service requirements of your customers. Whether a company produces a tangible product or sells professional services, all companies have a service aspect to their business. Taking orders, processing payables, and delivering goods are all services.

When performing services there are customer interfaces which will affect customer satisfaction. Responding to phone calls in a pleasant manner, resolving disputes or researching inquiries quickly are attributes of service quality. Good service quality results in customer satisfaction.

Some companies have taken a *service quality approach* rather than a process centered approach to quality improvement. A total quality program should include both service quality and process quality improvement efforts.

Voice of the Customer

What is the voice of the customer? If customers spoke directly to management what would they say? When referring to the voice of the customer (VOC) we are generally discussing customer needs and desires.

Many companies get customer information from warrantee cards, service calls, and complaints. This negative information only provides part of the information required to correctly gauge customer needs. Negative information only tells companies what customers do not want.

Quality oriented companies have sophisticated systems designed to gather positive customer information. Customer orientation dictates determining what will delight your customers.

Voice of the Customer Analysis

VOC analysis is a structured method for documenting the customer requirements for a product or service.

VOC analysis should be performed early in a process redesign project and then periodically to maintain a current awareness of customer requirements. A VOC team can be formed to perform the analysis at the same time a company defines its processes. However, the initial analysis should be completed before processes are redesigned or measurement criteria established. The results of the VOC analysis will influence the selection of measurement criteria and impact the decision of how to redesign processes.

Performing VOC analysis answers six basic questions about a product or service:

- Who is the customer?
- What is our product?
- When will it be used?
- Where will it be used?
- Why is it being used or chosen?
- How will it be used?

VOC analysis is a powerful tool that can be utilized for most products or services. As such, the specific tools and procedures utilized will vary based upon the nature of your industry.

Steps in performing Voice of the Customer Analysis

The methodology for VOC analysis is comprised of three basic steps:

❶ Planning the analysis
❷ Gathering customer information
❸ Evaluating customer information

❶ **Planning the analysis** - The first step in planning the VOC analysis is identification of customers. This step may be performed in conjunction with **process activity analysis**, or as an activity of the VOC team using tools such as **process maps, functional business models, information usage models**, or **brainstorming** techniques.

During the planning phase you also determine how information is to be gathered. Based upon the data gathering technique or techniques selected, determination of data evaluation methods may be performed at this stage. Sometimes it is useful to determine evaluation methods in advance to ensure that the correct type and volume of data is collected.

❷ **Data gathering** - Potential data gathering sources include:

- Magazines and periodicals
- Market research such as surveys, focus groups or interviews, etc.
- Point of sale information
- Warrantee data
- Government reports
- Internal perceptions

❸ **Data evaluation** - Data evaluation techniques include:

- **Voice of the Customer Tables**
- Statistical analysis
- Subjective analysis
- **Quality Function Deployment**

A combination of techniques may be required based upon the quantity, subjectivity and other factors affecting the data collected. Statistical analysis is extremely useful for determining attribute importance (see Tips below). Subjective analysis includes this use of tools such as **Force Field Analysis** and **Multi-voting**.

Voice of the Customer Tables

Voice of the Customer Tables are templates used to organize the information gathered from the customer.

I.D.	I/E	Customer(Who)	What?	When?	Where?	Why?	How?

Table 6-1

I.D.	=	Some identification # with which a customer can be tracked
I/E	=	Internal or External customer designation
Customer (Who)	=	An identification of the type or position of the customer and not necessarily the customer name.
What, When, Where, Why and How	=	The usage of the product or service. What is it used for, when is it used, where it is used, why was it chosen or used, and how was it used?

This information can then be aggregated or segregated in various ways. For example, the information could be analyzed using check sheets. A check sheet is a tool used to simplify data collection and analysis.

Characteristic	Count for attribute	Total
Mathematical error	IIIIIIIII	9
Improper P.O. #	IIII	4
No Approval	II	2
etc.		

Table 6-2

The information could be summarized into product or service characteristics. For example, through customer focus groups, we could have determined that the following are general characteristics according to which our product will be judged.

I.D.	Voice of the Customer	Demanded Quality	Accuracy	Timeliness	Comments

Table 6-3

Tips

> Include the market research department on your VOC team. They can usually streamline the data gathering and evaluation steps. The market research department may have answers to some of the questions regarding customer requirements. However, beware of a market researcher who "already has all the answers."

> Direct customer input is generally more reliable than internal perceptions. However, customers do not always say what they mean. For instance:

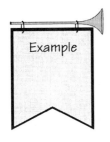

Example

A beer drinker might say that they purchase a particular brand due to the taste -- when they really buy based on peer influences or effective advertising and promotion.

Statistical tools are extremely useful for deriving attribute importance. Bi-variate correlation or multi-variate analysis (such as regression or factor analysis) can help determine the true influences.

When gathering data, include the entire customer population.

Beware of aggregating all customers into one category. Different consumer groups may purchase for vastly different reasons.

Outcome

After VOC analysis you will have defined the customer requirements and relative importance of product or service attributes. This information is required to implement a service quality program and to begin quality planning using tools such as **Quality Function Deployment**.

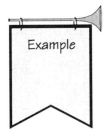

Example

The ABC Grocery Store has recently performed VOC analysis to better improve their sales and marketing techniques. ABC chose to question a representative sampling of customers as they entered the store to determine what they purchased, when they came, where they were from and why they chose ABC.

I.D.	I/E	Customer	What?	When?	Where?	Why?	Comments
1	E	Housewife - 36	Groceries, prescriptions	2x per week daytime	≈ 3 miles	Convenience, large store, variety of brands	Like pharmacist
2	E	Housewife - 54	Groceries, cosmetics, prescriptions	4x per week daytime	less than 1 mile	Convenience, knows register personnel, knows store layout	Only shops at ABC
3	E	Working mother - 29	Groceries, baby products	1x per week after work	≈ 5 miles	Double coupons, store brands	Goes where sales
4	E	Single Male - 23	Groceries, beer	Every other week	≈ 3 miles	Closest to apt., good beer selection	
5	E	Working father - 42	Groceries, rental movies	On way home - periodically	≈ 8 miles	On way home from work, movie rental dept.	Would like 3 day rather than 24 hr. rent
6	E	Single female - 29	Baked goods	1x per week	≈ 5 miles	Fresh bread	Gets fruits & vegetables from farmers market, wants organics
		etc...					

Table 6-4

This information was then organized by topic and summarized with a check sheet. The following represents why customers chose ABC by demographic group.

	Female Shoppers		Male Shoppers		
Customer Requirement	Married	Single	Married	Single	Total
Convenience	15	12	13	8	48
Variety	6	6	7	4	23
Sales circular/advertisements	8	6	4	0	18
Double coupons	8	5	4	0	17
Customer service	5	2	2	0	9
Movie department	3	2	3	1	9
etc.					
TOTAL SAMPLE SIZE	25	20	15	10	70

Table 6-5

The information could further be summarized by customer requirements as follows:

Voice of the Customer	ID	Demanded Quality		Quality Characteristics	
		Products	**Services**	**Products**	**Services**
Shop for convenience and for prescriptions	1	Pharmacy	Location		Personal touch
Convenience and customer service	2	Store layout			Personal touch
Pricing important	3		Low prices	Generics	Sales
Close and variety	4			Variety	
Convenience	5	Movie rental		Rent period	
etc...					

Table 6-6

Exercise

Using the list of customers identified in the exercise from Chapter 3 and the VOC table #1 from the appendix, perform a VOC analysis based upon your beliefs of customer needs.

Have other members of your organization perform the same analysis without showing them your's or each other's. Compare the internal perceptions. If possible, get external customer information (external to your department or company) and organize it using the table.

You may be surprised by the differences in perceptions between internal and external sources. The variances may be predictable but should indicate a course of action for your company.

Quality Function Deployment

Quality Function Deployment (QFD), commonly known as the house of quality, is a technique for identifying and translating the voice of the customer into plans and actions through each phase of product or service development.   The house of quality offers a systematic way to analyze the relationship between customer requirements, process characteristics and competitive rankings in a pictorial fashion.

After completing the initial VOC analysis, QFD can be utilized throughout a quality improvement effort, from the product or service planning phases through implementation, for both macro and micro processes. Some companies use QFD as the structure for their quality improvement program. Figure 6-2 depicts a QFD approach for the use of a series of four QFD matrices to translate customer requirements to process requirements in a service environment.

QFD takes the answers derived in VOC analysis and converts the information into action plans through a matrix analysis.

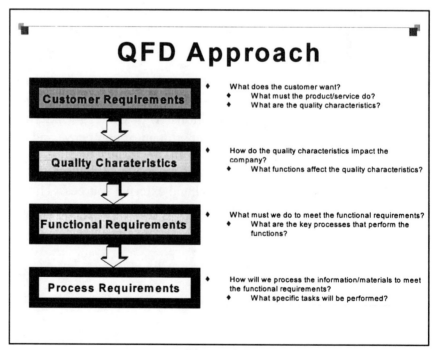

Figure 6-2

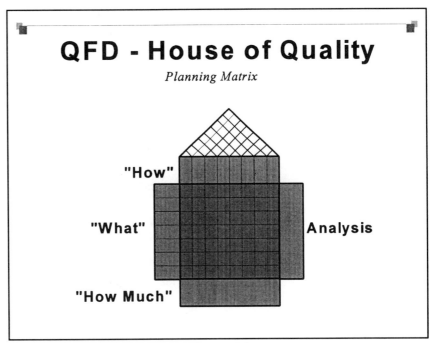

Figure 6-3

The QFD planning matrix charts customer, product, service, reliability, quality or other attributes; and evaluates the importance of those attributes within specified constraints.

QFD analysis can be extremely thorough and complicated when being used to its fullest advantage. QFD concepts can be applied in simpler terms to provide insights into processes. There are seven basic steps in performing QFD regardless of the depth of the analysis.

❶   Select Attribute
❷   Answer WHAT?
❸   Answer HOW?
❹   Compare relationship between WHAT and HOW
❺   Compare relationship between HOWs
❻   Answer HOW MUCH?
❼   Competitive and target analysis

❶   **Select Attribute** - The first question in any QFD analysis is, "What does the customer want?" The customer wants a product or service that has many attributes. The depth of the analysis and sophistication of the group performing QFD will influence the attribute selected for study.

A first attempt at QFD should select a broad description for the analysis. The example in this chapter is that of a producer of soft drinks. The attribute selected is the basic customer need - a refreshing soft drink.

❷   **Answer WHAT?** Development of the house of quality begins in the "WHAT" room. WHAT's refer to the list of customer requirements as determined in the VOC analysis or simply, what is to be achieved.

These are usually listed in order of customer importance. As demonstrated in Figure 6-4, the WHAT's being analyzed could be a subset of the customer requirements. In this case, a refreshing soft drink was one of the customer requirements. Other desirable attributes might be that the drink keeps them awake or has few calories.

❸   **Answer HOW?** - Next the "HOW" room is filled with methods for satisfying the customer requirements. The HOW's should consist of items that your company can measure and control. Measurement and control are vital to ensure that you can manipulate the HOW' to achieve customer satisfaction and delight.

❹   **Compare relationship between WHAT and HOW** - The relationship between the WHAT's and the HOW's is then plotted as identified in Figure 6-6. Notice that the relationship matrix uses simple measures of correlation - weak, medium, and strong.

❺ **Compare relationship between HOW's** - Next, the inter-relationships between the HOW's is plotted in the roof of the house of quality (Figure 6-7).

If two HOW's help each other improve the probability of customer satisfaction, they are considered to have a positive or strong positive relationship. If one HOW makes it more difficult to meet the target of another HOW, then they are considered to have a negative or strong negative relationship.

❻ **Answer HOW MUCH?** - Target values are determined where possible for the HOW values and included in the "HOW MUCH" room. It is common to also add values of your current product and competitive products in the room.

This level of analysis may be sufficient to analyze the relationships and determine where improvement is most needed. Sometimes action plans are then developed using subjective tools such as **Multi-voting** or **Force Field Analysis**.

❼ **Competitive and target analysis** - If additional information is required for decision-making, an expanded house of quality can be developed. A competitive analysis or WHY room can be added to describe how the customer perceives various market influences. These WHY's can then be plotted versus the WHAT's to help determine which WHAT's need to be improved first.

HOW's can also be plotted versus HOW MUCH's to determine the relative importance of each HOW and to help establish realistic targets for future products and services.

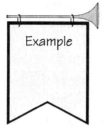

Example

A soft drink company decided to use QFD to analyze how it sold its products. The initial analysis was performed at a macro level to answer the question, "What characteristics should our products have to meet the customer's need for a refreshing soft drink?"

The company employed a cross-functional team of marketing, sales, distribution and production personnel to develop the QFD analysis.

The team's first task was to determine the characteristics of a drink that make it "refreshing." The team used the question, "How do customers define refreshing?" Figure 6-4 was developed based upon both internal perceptions and external information supplied by the marketing department.

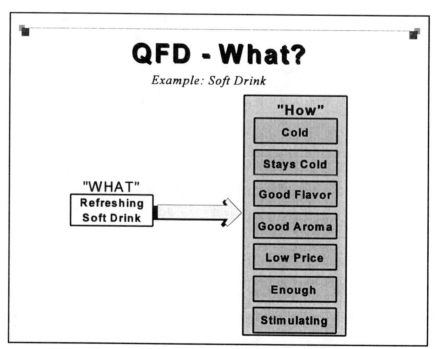

Figure 6-4

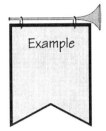

Example

The team then developed Figure 6-5 indicating how the company meets those needs identified in the WHAT.

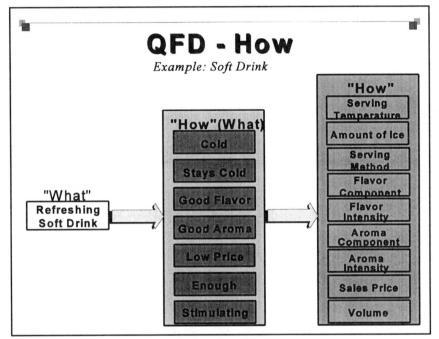

Figure 6-5

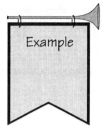

Example

The team then began its evaluation of the interrelationships between the WHAT versus HOW as depicted in Figure 6-6. They chose simple measures of correlation (strong, medium, and weak) due to the broad nature of the analysis and the desire to reach consensus on all decisions.

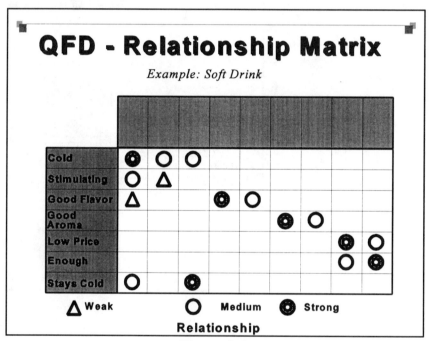

Figure 6-6

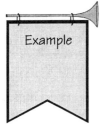

Example

The team then developed initial estimates of HOW MUCH based upon information from the sales and distribution departments. HOW's for which no empirical data was available are shown as Figure 6-7. The team decided that further research should be performed, but did not want the detail to stall their progress.

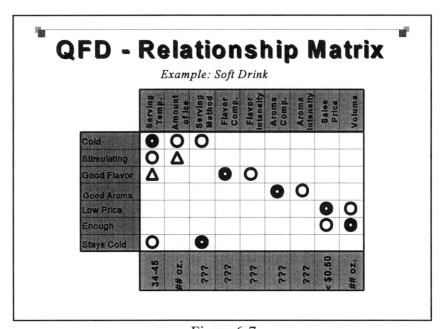

Figure 6-7

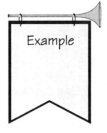

Example

The roof of the house of quality was then added to assess the interrelationships between HOW's.

The team had difficulty reaching consensus on what would be considered a positive impact versus a negative impact for each HOW. For example, a lower serving temperature was considered better, thus more positive. A more difficult question to answer was, "Is a higher price positive or negative?" Up to 50¢ may be positive, but after that, price increases were negative to the customer. These issues were resolved prior to assessing impact.

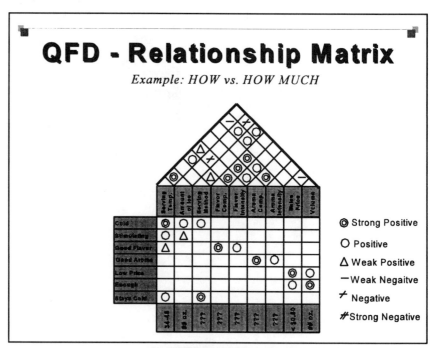

Figure 6-8

Tips

✑ Keep the size of the QFD matrix manageable. There may be hundreds of customer requirements or ways to satisfy them, but the larger the matrix, the more difficult the analysis and the more muddled the answers become. If you have 20 customer requirements and 50 ways to affect those requirements, 1000 WHAT versus HOW relationships must be analyzed!

✑ Try to identify the key factors for analysis. If all factors *must* be analyzed, segregate them into smaller matrices if possible. Potential segregation techniques include market segment or groups of similar customer requirements.

✑ There is good software available. In addition to creating clean, artistic representations of the QFD matrix as it evolves, computerized packages can help analyze the information. Software can take customer importance rankings, changeability factors, competitive analysis and other information and calculate overall importance factors. These factors can then be updated automatically as newer, more accurate information or new HOW's or WHAT's are introduced.

✑ Use market research or other data gathering techniques to further define critical customer requirements as they are identified. QFD is a learning experience which will require more information as you progress.

Outcome

After QFD you will have credible and compelling information to guide the plans and actions of the quality improvement effort.

Exercise

In Chapter 7 there will be an exercise for Cause and Effect Diagrams to help analyze how you can please your immediate supervisor (the customer) by getting to work earlier in the morning. After completing that exercise, use the QFD matrix below to evaluate alternative actions. If you are already a morning person, use the matrix to evaluate how you can motivate your employees to get to work earlier.

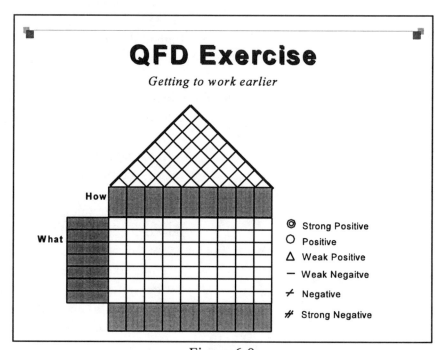

Figure 6-9

CHAPTER 7

Problem Solving and Decision Making Tools

Chapter Objectives

Process redesign and management are business strategies that are intended to result in improved corporate performance. Like any other strategy, there must be specific actions to make those strategies reality.

This chapter focuses on team problem solving and decision making tools. These tools are the basis for action taken in a quality improvement or reengineering effort. Specific chapter objectives include:

☞ Explain problem solving and decision making in a process orientation; and

☞ Provide specific tools for determining root cause and making team decisions.

Each tool is defined, demonstrated, explained and placed in the context of an overall redesign program.

Problem Solving Tools

Redesign teams will use problem solving tools to analyze information for informed decision making. These tools organize information so that it is more readily understood.

Problem solving is a process that follows certain procedures. In order to understand the function and use of problem solving tools it is useful to review the steps involved.

❶ Define the problem
❷ Determine the root cause of the problem
❸ Identify possible solutions
❹ Determine the best solution

❶ **Define the problem** - The first step in solving any problem is problem definition. Without a clear understanding of the problem and consensus among team members on that understanding, problem solving should not begin.

❷ **Determine the root cause of the problem** - Too often in the business world the focus of problems is on blame and short-term solutions (Figure 7-1). Without looking for the root cause we treat the symptoms and not the disease (Figure 7-2).

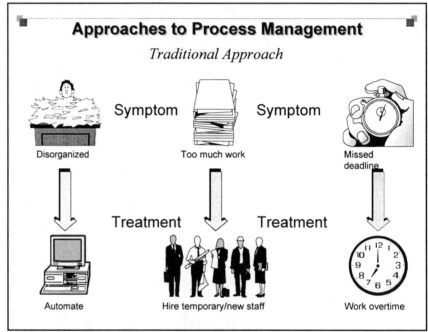

Figure 7-1

❸ **Identify possible solutions** - Once the root causes have been identified, it is time to search for possible solutions. Often managers believe they "*know*" their processes and assume that they also "*know*" the answers to process problems. As discussed in Chapter 5, the best answer is not always the most apparent answer.

❹ **Determine the best solution** - Choosing the best solution requires effort, honesty, persistence, patience and facts. The *best* solution may not be readily determined the first time a problem is analyzed.

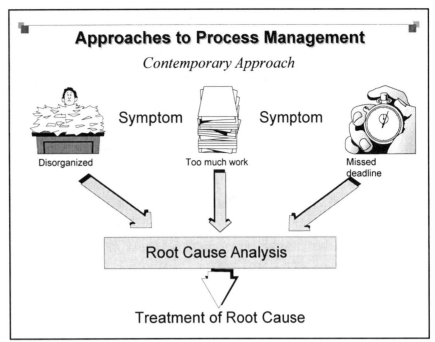

Figure 7-2

Root Cause Determination

Cause and Effect Diagrams

Cause and effect diagrams, also known as fishbone diagrams due to their shape, and Ishikawa diagrams named after the man who first used them, are one of the primary problem solving tools used by quality improvement teams. Cause and effect diagrams are flexible and can be used in a variety of circumstances. As such, they are one of the most powerful problem solving tools.

Cause and effect diagrams are used to systematically explore the possible causes of problems and to identify the true cause or causes. These charts are often associated with the evaluation of a negative condition (i.e., causes of defects). The tool is also very effective for identifying the causes of peak performance (i.e., what symptoms or indicators created success) or determining a possible solution.

When searching for the solution to a problem, the identified causes are in essence answering the question, "Why is this happening?" When searching for a positive outcome, the identified causes are answering the question, "How can I achieve this end result again?"

Steps in Creating a Cause and Effect Diagram

There are six steps in creating a cause and effect diagram:

❶   Identify the outcome to be analyzed
❷   Draw a "fishbone" diagram
❸   Determine the major categories of causes
❹   Brainstorm for all possible causes
❺   Evaluate the causes
❻   Rank the causes

❶   **Identify the outcome to be analyzed** - It is vital that all team members have a common understanding of the outcome being analyzed. In some circumstances the outcome may be broad in scope and easy to comprehend. As the team progresses, they might take one of the causes and further analyze it to determine more detailed causes. Generally, the more specific the outcome, the more useful the chart will be.

❷   **Draw a "fishbone" diagram** - Cause and effect diagrams are commonly called fishbone charts due to their appearance. The head of the fish is a large box in which the effect is written. The body of the fish is drawn as a skeleton (Figure 7-3).

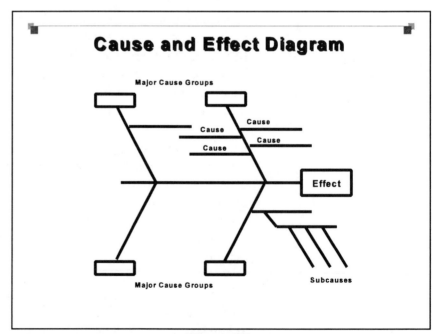

Figure 7-3

❸ **Determine the major categories of causes** - Four to six major categories are used to group the root causes. These categories are the broad classifications describing the causes that impact your outcome. Often used as starting categories are the four P's: People; Procedures; Policies; and Plant. In an office environment, the category "plant" is often replaced by "equipment" or "technology."

❹ **Brainstorm for all possible causes** - With the major categories as a guide, determine as many causes of the outcome or effect being studied as possible. Each cause is a bone on the fish. Subcauses are indicated as branches off the cause to which they relate.

❺ **Evaluate the causes** - Once all of the causes are listed, evaluate them and circle those most common and important.

❻ **Rank the causes** - Finally, rank the circled causes in order of importance. Be sure that all team members have aired their opinions and that the pros and cons have been thoroughly discussed.

Tips

☞ When you are brainstorming for root causes, focus on one major category at a time. By structuring the brainstorming activity, it is more likely that the category will be fully analyzed. If ideas come up that fit other categories or suggest a new category, write it down. Incorporate the new category if necessary, but return to the category being discussed to be sure all causes in that category are discovered and/or identified.

☞ After brainstorming, the group may wish to suspend the analysis until the next meeting to allow time for the initial analysis to incubate. When the next meeting begins, review the chart and see if there are any more causes to be added before evaluating existing causes.

✏ Consider the use of *multi-voting* or *nominal group technique* or other consensus tools (Chapter 5) when ranking the causes. For example, cause and effect analysis can be useful in determining a course of action or priority of efforts. In this case, consensus on the ranking of causes is imperative.

✏ Cause and effect diagrams can also be used for a variety of purposes other than documenting the causes of historical problems or successes.

• *An outlining tool* - Instead of brainstorming for causes, use the fishbone diagram as a method to record the outcomes of a brainstorming session.

• *Blank slate redesign* - Blank slate redesign is determining a proposed process without the bias of the existing system. The outcome or effect could be the *perfect system*; the categories the major components; and the bones the details of the system.

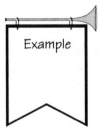

Example

The manager of the corporate cafeteria noticed an increase in the amount of excess food left over after lunch. The excess food was obviously a waste of the limited resources in his budget. Together with a team of cooks, servers, and bus persons the cause and effect chart in Figure 7-4 was developed.

After developing the chart, a questionnaire was circulated to cafeteria customers to determine the primary causes. Additional causes were also determined from interviews with selected customers. It was determined that food prepared in bulk prior to lunch lost its appeal to late lunch customers. Varying the amount of food prepared was crucial as certain meals proved more popular than others. In addition, the vegetable selection and grouping with main entrees had a great impact on the amount of food purchased.

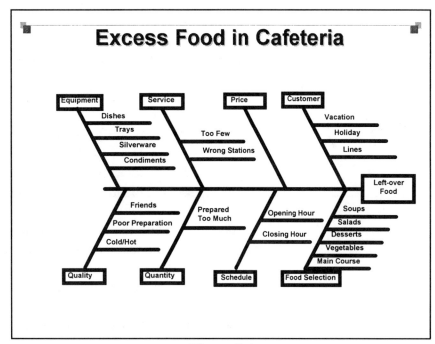

Figure 7-4

Exercise

Using a blank cause and effect form located in the Appendix, create a cause and effect diagram to determine how you can get to work earlier each morning. Either prepare it in search of the reason why you are late; or if you are an early bird, for potential ways to improve your morning routine to get you to work even earlier.

Force Field Analysis

Force Field Analysis is a tool used to graphically depict the pros and cons in a given situation or proposed solution. Force Field Analysis is used to identify those forces that help and hinder closing the gap between where you are now and where you want to be. It includes the assessment of relative strengths of those forces and aids in judging the total force on a given situation or solution.

In a given situation, status quo is maintained due to various opposing forces. These forces act as counterbalances that maintain the current situation. A Force Field Analysis can be used to identify those forces, and their relative strengths, in order to facilitate change.

Steps in Creating a Force Field Analysis

There are steps in creating a Force Field Analysis:

    ❶   Identify the issue being analyzed
    ❷   Draw the Force Field diagram
    ❸   Identify the positive forces
    ❹   Identify the opposing forces

❶   **Identify the issue being analyzed** - As in most problem solving methods, identifying and defining the problem is half of the solution. Ensure that all team members are in agreement on the situation or problem being analyzed.

❷   **Draw the Force Field diagram** - On a flip chart or white board draw a large T chart as illustrated in Figure 7-5. Then draw another vertical line near the right edge of the page. The ideal state of the situation or purpose of the chart should be written on top of the T on the far right of the diagram.

❸   **Identify the positive forces** - Brainstorm for all of the positive forces, both internal and external, that drive the organization toward the goal or purpose being analyzed. List these forces to the left of the T on the chart. Under each force, draw arrows that represent the force's relative strength.

❹   **Identify the opposing forces** - Brainstorm for all of the forces, both internal and external, that impede the organization from achieving the goal. List these forces to the right of the center line and draw arrows indicating their relative strength.

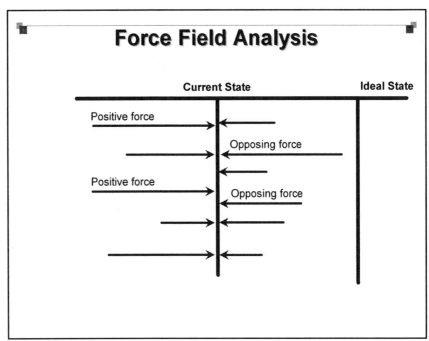

Figure 7-5

Tips

✏ Force Field Analysis is non-scientific in nature. The ranking of forces is generally performed subjectively and can be heavily influenced by the opinions of one or more individuals in a group. As such, you should not rely on Force Field Analysis for "answers," but rather as a method to focus the efforts of a team.

✏ It is often helpful to assess the relative strengths of the opposing forces using a numerical scale. For example, a ranking of one through five may be assigned for evaluating the relative strengths of forces such as:

>   5 = Very strong
>   4 = Strong
>   3 = Moderate
>   2 = Weak
>   1 = Wimpy

This scaling will also aid in graphically depicting the strengths as proportionally sized arrows.

✏ To increase the usefulness of the chart, some teams list descriptors of the forces in their ideal state to the right of the chart beyond a second vertical line. Additionally, you may wish to indicate factors that influence the various forces or note where information regarding the force can be obtained on the left hand side of the chart. This additional information can be useful when returning to the chart at a later date. However, when making presentations, avoid a chart that is cluttered with too much information.

✏ After developing the chart, your group can use the information to develop possible solutions. Some ideas the group can explore include:

- How to increase the number or strength of positive forces; and

- How to decrease the number or strength of hindering forces.

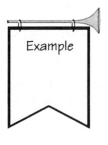
Example

The CEO of a professional service firm chartered a team to create a continuous quality improvement program throughout the organization. After several months little success was evident other than a few small projects. The team decided a Force Field Analysis should be performed to identify the factors helping and hindering their program.

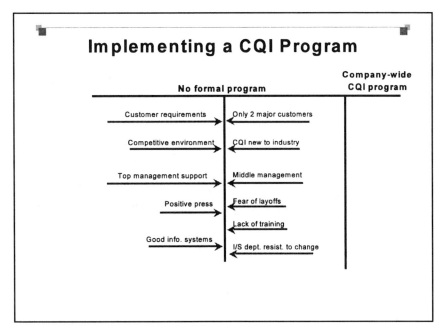

Figure 7-6

Exercise

Create a Force Field Analysis for the forces affecting your quality improvement program. Consider the political, resource and cost constraints in your analysis. Then take one of the biggest forces and perform a Force Field Analysis on that constraint.

Pareto Analysis

Pareto analysis is a tool used to prioritize data by graphically depicting information about a process by frequency of occurrence of some event. The technique uses a modified histogram (Chapter 8) in which the frequency of problems is plotted relative to their causes.

Pareto analysis is based upon the theory that 20% of the effort produces 80% of the results, or conversely that 80% of the problems are created by 20% of the causes. If this is true, work can be prioritized to focus on the 20% that creates the greatest results. The pareto principle is often called the 80-20 rule; "80% of our business comes from 20% of our customers."

The graphical representation of a Pareto Chart enables group members to clearly identify the problems that create the most negative effects.

Steps in Creating a Pareto Analysis

There are nine steps in performing a Pareto Analysis:

❶ Collect and record data
❷ Arrange the data by frequency of occurrence
❸ Sum all occurrences
❹ Calculate the percentage for each category
❺ Calculate the cumulative percentage
❻ Draw the Pareto Chart
❼ Scale the chart
❽ Plot and draw the columns
❾ Plot the cumulative line

❶ **Collect and record data** - A Pareto Analysis is not a data gathering tool. Data on the process or procedure being analyzed must be gathered prior to construction of the chart. A check sheet (Chapter 8) is a useful tool for gathering information to be portrayed in a Pareto Analysis.

❷ **Arrange the data by frequency of occurrence** - The data collected in step one should be categorized. Each category should be totaled to determine the order of the columns on the Pareto Chart. The categories should be arranged in descending order.

❸ **Sum all occurrences** - All categories are totaled for purposes of determining the percentage attributed to each cause.

❹ **Calculate the percentage for each category** - The total of each category is then divided by the sum of all occurrences. This fraction is depicted as a percentage on the Pareto Chart.

❺   **Calculate the cumulative percentage** - The cause categories have been arranged in descending order and percentages have been calculated for each cause. The cumulative percentage is calculated by adding the total of the current category with those of the larger categories previously analyzed.

❻   **Draw the Pareto Chart** - A Pareto Chart can easily be drawn with a piece of graph paper. The causes will be represented by vertical bars along the horizontal axis.

❼   **Scale the chart** - We recommend scaling the vertical axis using both the frequency and percentage of occurrence. In Figure 7-7 the total number of occurrences is along the left axis and the percentage of occurrence appears beside the right vertical axis.

❽   **Plot and draw the columns** - In descending order, place bar columns to represent each cause category.

❾   **Plot the cumulative line** - The cumulative line shows the total number of occurrences for each column until all occurrences have been accounted for.

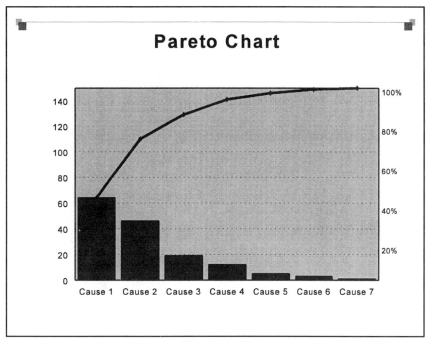

Figure 7-7

Tips

✏   The process of constructing a Pareto Chart is simpler than it appears, especially considering it can be performed automatically by computer in a wide assortment of application software. In addition to statistical analysis software packages, Pareto Charts can be generated by most spreadsheet, word processing or presentation software.

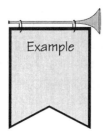

A manufacturing company charges labor hours to jobs for costing purposes. Sales and operations managers know from analysis of the job cost reports that labor costs are not being properly applied to jobs. The following is a Pareto Analysis of the causes of erroneous labor reporting.

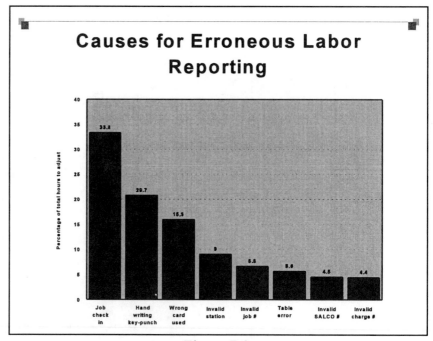

Figure 7-8

Exercise

Using the following data, construct a Pareto Chart:

Reason Late to Work Last Month	#	%	Cum
Traffic	12		
Up late previous night	8		
Bad hair day	3		
Alarm set for PM	2		
Spouse frisky	1		

Table 7-1

Decision Making Tools

Often process improvement teams make great strides at determining the root causes of problems, but have difficulty determining which causes are most important. Or, they may have difficulty reaching a consensus when evaluating solutions.

Decision making is also a process that follows a progression. To effectively utilize the decision making tools, first review the steps in decision making.

❶ Identify the decision criteria
❷ Analyze solutions versus the criteria
❸ Reach a consensus

❶ **Identify the decision criteria** - During the problem solving process, the redesign team may have determined several causes of inefficiency. When selecting a solution, the various alternatives may cure one cause and not another. These cures generally become the criteria by which a decision is made. Figure 7-9 lists several common decision criteria.

Decision Criteria

- Impact on problem
  - Time savings
  - Material savings
  - Effect on morale
  - # of people who benefit
  - Safeguarding of data/resources
- Changeability
  - Decision making levels required
  - Complexity of investigation
  - Estimated time to solve/implement
  - Ability to measure
  - Resource requirements

- Depending upon the problem sub-headings may become major criteria

Figure 7-9

❷　**Analyze solutions versus the criteria** - The focus of this section of the chapter is techniques for analyzing alternative solutions.

❸　**Reach a consensus** - Without consensus among team members, implementation of the plan may be compromised. Use of the decision making tools described below help build a consensus among team members. Specific consensus building tools are discussed in Chapter 5.

Four commonly used decision making tools are:

- Priority Assessment
- Criteria Rating Forms
- Multi-Voting
- Matrix Analysis

Priority Assessment

One common challenge is prioritizing tasks. Should a team tackle the monumental tasks first or accomplish smaller, more attainable goals first? In what order should similar size tasks be undertaken?

A simple analysis of priority assessment for possible solutions or task ordering based upon two decision criteria, impact and chargeability, is identified in Figure 7-9. **Impact** refers to the effect on the problem the given solution may have. Impact can also be the effect on the total project a particular task may have. **Changeability** refers to the level of effort required to impose a particular solution or complete a given task.

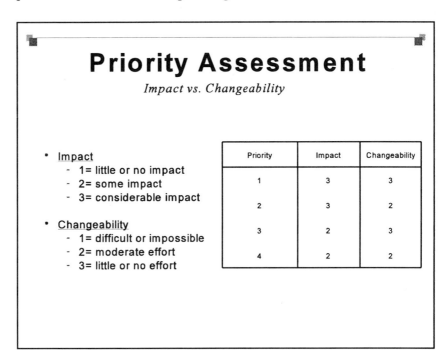

Priority Assessment
Impact vs. Changeability

* Impact
  - 1= little or no impact
  - 2= some impact
  - 3= considerable impact

* Changeability
  - 1= difficult or impossible
  - 2= moderate effort
  - 3= little or no effort

Priority	Impact	Changeability
1	3	3
2	3	2
3	2	3
4	2	2

Figure 7-10

Criteria Rating Forms

A criteria rating form is a tool to display information comparing options against each other and against established criteria. Figure 7-10 illustrates a table by which teams can judge how to prioritize their activities. This priority assessment tool is a simple version of a criteria rating form. Team members can vote on, or agree on, rankings from one to three for each task or solution.

Criteria rating forms are used to list problems, solutions, or options on one axis, and the criteria being used for evaluation on the other axis. A simple rating (on a scale of 1 to 5, for instance) of the relative strength of each option can be determined. If the relative importance of each criteria is equal, a simple addition of all the ratings for identified criteria, by solution, can be used to aid in decision making.

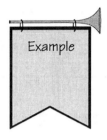

Example

John Q. Public, CPA is trying to determine the best way to assign individual tax returns among preparers at his CPA firm. A process improvement team has determined several criteria upon which to base its decision. The initial analysis is depicted in Table 7-2.

Criteria Rating Form
Decision = Tax Return Stratification System

Criteria	Options			
	Tax Pool	Tax Team	Assignment	Immediate Prep
Impact on Client Service	1	2	3	3
Time Required for Implementation	3	3	1	1
Cost to Change	3	3	2	1
Process Simplification	3	3	2	1
Total	10	11	8	6

Table 7-2

Criteria rating becomes more powerful when each criteria is weighted for relative importance in the decision making process. Each criteria may have different relative importance to different departments within a company or individuals on a team. Weighting of criteria can also have a dramatic impact on the results of the analysis.

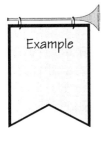
Example

Mr. Public reviewed the analysis of the team and felt that the decision process was too simplistic and that the other partners in the firm should provide input on the relative importance of each decision criteria.

The team also decided that the decision for each rating should be more clearly defined, and developed a scale for each option on which to determine the votes. The scale was changed from 1-3 to 1-5.

The team reconsidered its decision based upon the input of the partners and developed the criteria rating form depicted in Table 7-3.

Criteria Rating Form
Decision = Tax Return Stratification System

Criteria	Options				
	Weight	Tax Pool	Tax Teams	Assignment	Immediate Prep
Impact on Client Service 0%|--------------------|5% Estimated increase in customer satisfaction	3	0 / 0	2 / 6	3 / 9	4 / 12
Time Required for Implementation 0|----------3------------|5 >1yr 6mos 1mo	2	5 / 10	5 / 10	1 / 2	0 / 0
Cost to Change 0|-----------|-----------|5 $50K $0	1	5 / 5	4 / 4	1 / 1	0 / 0
Process Simplification 0|----------------------|5 None Drastic	1	0 / 0	2 / 2	1 / 1	3 / 3
Total Score		15	22	13	15

Table 7-3

Tips

✏ Criteria rating can be more or less subjective depending upon the amount of data analysis performed and the detail of the criteria rating analysis. The greater the use of data and objectivity, the more powerful the tool becomes.

✏ Criteria rating should be used to **influence** decisions and not to make them. If the criteria rating analysis results in an unexpected outcome, the team may wish to review the initial analysis rather than accept the results.

Multi-Voting

When team members cannot agree on rankings such as impact or changeability, multi-voting provides a method for capturing input of all members and creating a composite vote for the team. Votes of each member are recorded without trying to reach consensus on a particular rating value.

Each team member is given a number of votes to distribute among the various solution alternatives in accordance with their preferences. Members then distribute their votes among the various options to indicate their relative preferences.

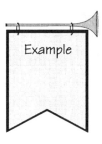

Example

A team of six salespeople were debating how to apportion their marketing budget. The group narrowed their alternatives for the discretionary part of their budget to five choices. Each team member was given eight votes to allocate among the five choices. The votes were aggregated in Table 7-4. Based upon the results of the weighted voting, the group eliminated the alternatives of spending funds on mass mailings and collateral materials.

Alternative	Votes	Count
Collateral Material	IIII	4
Trade Shows	IIIII	5
Magazine Advertising	IIIIIIIIIIII	12
Increased T&E budget	IIIIIII	7
Mass mailing	II	2

Table 7-4

Tips

✏   Encourage people to spread their votes to represent their relative feelings rather than lumping all their votes on a single favorite.

✏   Have all team members write down their votes before any votes are recorded by the team scribe. Then have each member disclose their votes by option, not by person. By running down each option one at a time, it is easier to discern agreement and disagreement among team members.

✏   The result of multi-voting is information as to the relative *group think* about the various alternatives. It merely provides information about where individual members stand and how strongly. Opinions are quantified and revealed in an organized fashion. To reach a consensus and make a decision, the voting differences among members must be discussed and resolved.

✏   Multi-voting is most appropriate when the number of options is less than ten.

Matrix Analysis

Matrix analysis is an analytical tool for determining the interrelationships between criteria, options, solutions, etc. Applications of matrix analysis are far ranging. For example, matrix analysis can be used to develop a measure of the relative importance of decision criteria. A specific example of matrix analysis for a determination of customer needs is Quality Function Deployment explained in Chapter 6.

Steps in Creating a Matrix Analysis

There are four steps in creating a matrix analysis:

❶   Identify the alternatives to be analyzed
❷   Create a matrix for the number of alternatives
❸   Perform a paired comparison of the alternatives
❹   Compile the results of the comparison

❶ **Identify the alternatives to be analyzed** - The alternatives may be the key decision making criteria the customer needs, or potential solutions to a problem. The analysis should only be performed on the key alternatives well into the decision making process.

❷ **Create a matrix for the number of alternatives** - The matrix is a table of boxes with the number of rows and columns equal to the number of alternatives. The alternatives are listed down the left side and across the top of the matrix in the same order. The box at the intersection of the identical options is darkened. For some analyses, each remaining box may be subdivided for performing dual paired analyses on the same intersection of alternatives.

❸ **Perform a paired comparison of the alternatives** - Depending upon the type of matrix analysis performed, the comparison may result in a numeric or symbolic comparison of alternatives.

In the example of QFD in Chapter 6, symbols were used to represent the interrelationship between customer requirements and quality characteristics. In many instances, including QFD analysis, quantitative measures of relationship are used. For example, the following numerical values may be assigned:

-5	Strong negative relationship
-3	Moderate negative relationship
-1	Weak negative relationship
0	No relationship
1	Weak positive relationship
3	Moderate positive relationship
5	Strong positive relationship

The relative weights and categories of comparison differ based upon the type of analysis being performed.

❹ **Compile the results of the comparison** - Down the right side of the matrix the total of the row is aggregated. Other relative measures may also be displayed, such as:

- Relative percentage of the total score
- Competitive benchmarks
- Ideal state measurements

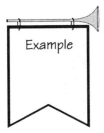
Example

A motorcycle sales and service shop recently came under new management. The managers believe that a variety of factors were leading to less than expected return on their investment. After brainstorming for ways to increase profitability, they derived the following list of alternative actions.

- Increase service department size and activity
- Increase sales of custom and pre-owned motorcycles
- Increase sales of retail parts and novelty items
- Improve customer service to obtain more repeat business
- Reduce prices to increase volume of sales
- Increase the margin on existing sales

These alternatives were evaluated in a decision criteria matrix to determine whether additional funds should be expended in advertising, expansion of the service department, or reorganization of sales and office staff.

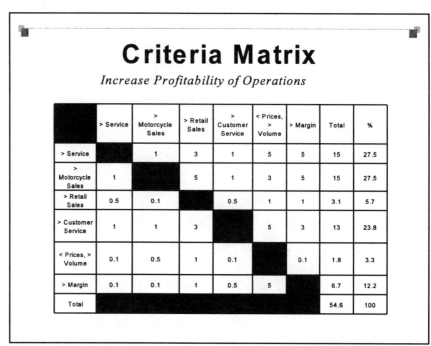

Criteria Matrix

Increase Profitability of Operations

	> Service	> Motorcycle Sales	> Retail Sales	> Customer Service	< Prices, > Volume	> Margin	Total	%
> Service		1	3	1	5	5	15	27.5
> Motorcycle Sales	1		5	1	3	5	15	27.5
> Retail Sales	0.5	0.1		0.5	1	1	3.1	5.7
> Customer Service	1	1	3		5	3	13	23.8
< Prices, > Volume	0.1	0.5	1	0.1		0.1	1.8	3.3
> Margin	0.1	0.1	1	0.5	5		6.7	12.2
Total							54.6	100

Figure 7-11

Example

The first matrix used (Figure 7-11) compared each of the six criteria with each other using a scale of :

5	Much more important
3	More important
1	Directly related or equally important
.5	Less important
.1	Much less important

The top three alternatives were compared against the three funding options using the same criteria (Figure 7-12).

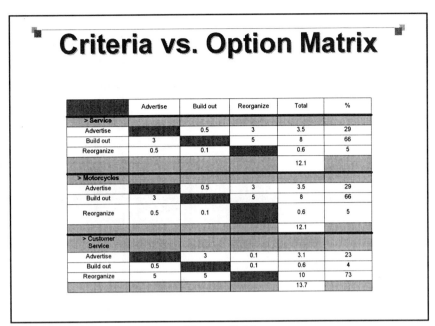

Figure 7-12

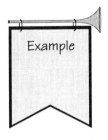

Example

The results of the two analyses were combined in a third matrix by multiplying the relative strengths of each alternative (their percentile scores) as shown in Figure 7-13.

Although the results of this exercise appeared obvious to some members of management, the process of choosing alternatives led to greater insights for all team members. Advertising may help boost the profitability of all areas, but its relative merit compared to improving customer service was less than expected.

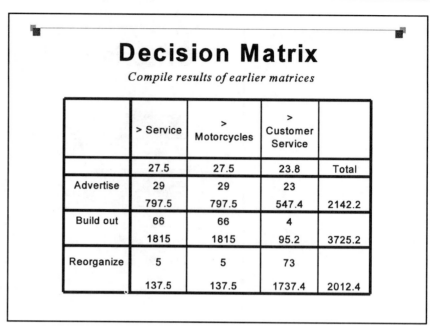

Decision Matrix

Compile results of earlier matrices

	> Service	> Motorcycles	> Customer Service	
	27.5	27.5	23.8	Total
Advertise	29	29	23	
	797.5	797.5	547.4	2142.2
Build out	66	66	4	
	1815	1815	95.2	3725.2
Reorganize	5	5	73	
	137.5	137.5	1737.4	2012.4

Figure 7-13

Tips

✏ Using a matrix analysis need not be as complex as the example of the motorcycle shop. A simple comparison may lead to some of the same types of insights as a more thorough evaluation.

✏ Creating matrices may appear complex, but the mechanics are relatively simple and can be performed without sophisticated software. With practice, the mechanics will become routine.

✏ Determine relative importance through consensus and not through voting. Without consensus, the results of the matrix can be questioned. With consensus on the relative importance of each criteria, the power of the matrix to move the team towards action will be substantial.

✏ The relationship between identical criteria should be reciprocal. Option A when compared to Option B should be the exact opposite of Option B compared to Option A. Some teams may wish to fill in the reciprocal value as soon as the first comparison is made. Other teams may wish to work across rows and use the second comparison as a consensus check.

CHAPTER 8

Statistical Process Control

Chapter Objectives

Statistical methods are proven tools to reduce nonconformance and improve process stability, productivity and quality. Through the use of statistical tools, businesses can focus on the causes of variation and concentrate their process improvement efforts on the elimination of problems *before they occur*.

This chapter focuses on the use of statistical concepts and control charts to improve processes. Specific chapter objectives include:

- ☞ Review some basic statistical concepts;
- ☞ Discuss data collection and presentation techniques; and
- ☞ Explain how to construct and use statistical process control charts.

Statistical Process Control (SPC) charts are widely applicable and easily implemented. We will demonstrate their usefulness through several examples.

Concepts

Variation is inevitable. No two products or services will be 100% identical every time they are produced or performed. In many instances, even the slightest variability can lead to a decrease in customer satisfaction. Testing for variation, or inspecting for quality of a product or service does not necessarily improve its inherent quality. SPC techniques can be used to analyze data from a process and draw conclusions taking variation into account so that the variation can be eliminated.

No matter how well a process is designed, there is a certain amount of inherent or natural variability. This natural variability may be caused by one or many essentially natural causes. A process that is operating with only natural or chance variation is said to be in statistical control.

Other causes of variability are generally caused by people, materials or equipment. These causes of variability are referred to as "assignable causes" because they can be traced to an input that is controllable. When a process is operating with assignable causes, it is deemed to be out of control.

SPC Tools

SPC can be applied to any process. SPC is most effective when used in a proactive manner to eliminate assignable causes of variation. The major SPC tools are:

❶	Histogram
❷	Check Sheet
❸	Pareto Chart
❹	Cause and Effect Diagram
❺	Defect Concentration Diagram
❻	Scatter Diagram
❼	Stem and Leaf Chart
❽	Control Chart

Many of these tools have been previously explained under the context of general process improvement tools. This chapter focuses on the use of control charts and their application for business process improvement.

Statistics is the art of making decisions about a population of data or a process based upon information from a sample of data. Once the decision or inference is made, statistics then measures the reliability of those inferences. It involves systematic methods for data collection, presentation and analysis.

Data Collection

Data contains information useful for understanding how a process or system works. For purposes of reducing the volume of work and cost of data collection, presentation and analysis; a subset or sample of information is generally chosen from the entirety of the data (the population).

There are a variety of sampling methods and techniques. Sampling methods are either statistical or nonstatistical. Statistical sampling techniques allow statistical inference to draw conclusions about the sample. The basic premise in statistical sampling is that the data selected is representative of the population.

The most frequently discussed data collection techniques are random, systematic and haphazard.

- *Random selection* encompasses those techniques in which each sample value is selected from the entire population in such a way that every possible sample has an equal chance of being selected.
- *Systematic selection* is a technique by where every Nth item is chosen from a population to be included in the sample. Systematic selection can be used with statistical sampling if one or more random start points are selected.
- *Haphazard selection* is a technique where the sample is chosen without conscious bias, but without a specific pattern. Haphazard selection generally means picking a sample without any specific approach to guide the selection process while trying to maintain an unbiased selection process. Although it may be random in nature, haphazard selection is inappropriate for statistical analysis.

The data itself can be categorized as attribute or variables data.

- *Attribute data* represent characteristics or classifications. Attribute data are used to estimate a proportion of items containing the attribute of interest. For example, attributes can include errors, defects, conformity, complaints, etc. These attributes are usually measured over a period of time or as a percentage of documents or products produced. The proportion of the attribute identified compared to the sample or population is referred to as the occurrence rate.

- *Variables data* represent numerical measurements. Data that are quantitative and measured on a numerical scale are variables data.

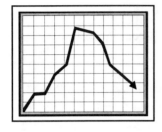

Data Presentation

Pictures are generally more intuitively descriptive and readily understood than words when presenting results of data collection. Most business managers are familiar with many presentation formats. Line, bar and pie charts are common in business applications. Among the seven major tools of SPC not previously covered in this workbook are the histogram, defect concentration diagram, scatter diagram and control chart.

Histograms

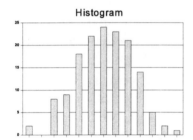

A Histogram is a form of bar chart showing the distribution of the sample data. Each bar represents a data value or range of values. The height of the bar is equal to the frequency of occurrence of each data point. The Histogram makes it easy to see the three properties of

- Shape,
- Central tendency, and
- Scatter of the data

in one visual representation.

Histograms are generally most useful for large samples. As each bar may represent a range of values and the selection of bars is subjective, Histograms are inappropriate for small samples. In recent years, Stem and Leaf Diagrams have replaced Histograms for visual representations of spread and central tendency in small samples.

Stem and Leaf Diagrams

Stem	Leaf	Frequency
0	5	1
1	5 8 0	3
2	1 0 3	3
3	4 1 3 5 3 5	6
4	2 9 5 8 3 1 6 9	8
5	4 7 1 3 4 0 8 8 6 8 0 8	12
6	3 0 7 3 0 5 0 8 7 9	10
7	8 5 4 4 1 6 2 1	8
8	0 3 6 1 4 1	6
9	9 6 0 9	4
10	7 1	2

Stem and Leaf Diagrams provide similar information to that of Histograms but have the added advantage of maintaining the specific values of each data point. In a Stem and Leaf Diagram, the stem is the first or several leading digits of the value of a data point and the leaf is the remaining digit.

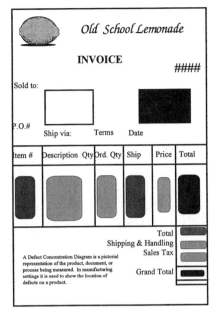

Defect Concentration Diagram

A Defect Concentration Diagram is a pictorial representation of the product, document, or process being measured. In manufacturing settings it is used to show the location of defects on a product. In a service setting it can be used to show where errors occurred on a document such as an invoice. The varying shades represent the concentration of errors in the various locations. On the sample invoice the most errors occurred in the "ship to," "total" and "grand total" areas of the document.

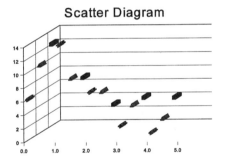

Scatter Diagram

A Scatter Diagram is a graphical display plotting the values of one variable *y* against the corresponding values of another variable *x*. The Scatter Diagram can provide information about the potential relationship between the two variables. Positive, negative or lack of relationship can easily be detected by looking at a scatter diagram. The three dimensional Scatter Diagram indicates a discernable pattern for the three variables represented.

Data Analysis

Statistical techniques enable business managers to analyze smaller samples of data for making decisions. Because small samples are used, the costs of decision making can also be reduced. In addition, statistical techniques can provide a measurement of risk associated with the analysis.

One important aspect of statistical analysis is the frequency distribution or shape of the data. Distribution shapes are depicted graphically as curves; and the probabilities that the variables take on particular values, is the area under the curve. The bell shaped curve, or normal distribution, is a very common shape. In the normal distribution, observations that are equidistant from the center of the curve have the same probability in the population (see Figure 8-1).

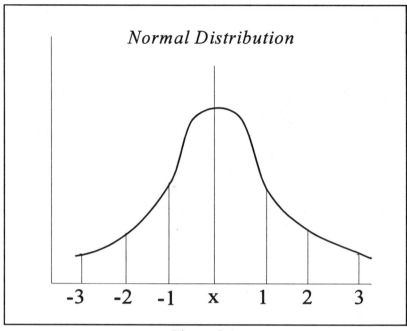

Figure 8-1

The **Central Limit Theorem** provides justification for the use of a normal distribution in many efforts involving data modeling and analysis. Regardless of the distribution of the individual observations in a population, the distribution of sample averages is always approximately normal. The larger the sample size, the more the distribution of the average will approximate the normal distribution.

The observations in a sample can be numerically described in a variety of ways.

- The spread between the largest and the smallest numerical values is called the **range**.

Numerical measurements that identify the center of the sample data are called measures of central tendency. These measurements allow for the creation of mental images of the data and the graphical representations of the data.

- The arithmetic average of all data points is called the **sample mean or sample average**. If we denote sample data points as $\times_1$, $\times_2$, ..., $\times_n$, the sample mean is defined as:

$$\bar{x} = \frac{\sum_{i=1}^{n} x_i}{n}$$

- The most frequently occurring data point is called the **mode**.
- The **median** is the data value that divides the sample exactly in half; that is, half the values are smaller than the median and half are larger.

In a normal distribution, the mean, the mode, and the median should be equal.

- The **variance** is a convenient measure of spread or variability on the data. It is denoted by the symbol s^2. The formula for the variance is:

$$s^2 = \frac{\sum_{i=1}^{n}(x_i - \bar{x})^2}{n - 1}$$

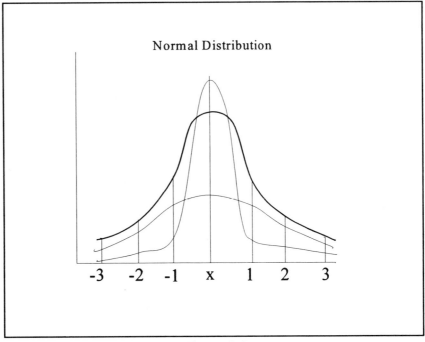

Figure 8-2

- The **standard deviation** is the most common measure of variation. The standard deviation is defined as the square root of the variance. The standard deviation of a sample is represented by the symbol s. Figure 8-2 shows normal distribution with different means and standard deviations.

Example

You are the agent for a baseball player and are trying to create a new way for calculating the pay of players based upon their batting average. You want to make certain assertions so you turn to statistical analysis for proof.

Assume that the mean batting average in the national league was .240 and that the standard deviation was .043. Your client hit .296 and management states that he is not a "superstar" since his average was below .300.

Using statistics you could demonstrate that your client's average is in the 91st percentile of all players and deserves to be paid accordingly.

In a normal distribution 62.86%, 95.46%, and 99.7% of all data points will fall within 1, 2, and 3 standard deviations from the mean, respectively. Using the standard deviation as a measure of variability around the mean allows you to measure the area under a normal distribution. This measurement can then be translated into a range of values. Alternatively, a range of values could be translated into a frequency distribution. Most basic statistics textbooks have tables to assist in performing these calculations. There are also a variety of computer software packages that can perform these calculations, and which support other types of statistical analysis.

Control Charts

Control Charts are graphical representations of samples of data taken over time. The goals of SPC and Control Charts specifically are:

❶   Measure stability over time
❷   Identify and remove assignable causes, thereby
      reducing variability
❸   Detect changes in the process

The typical Control Chart is comprised of a series of measurements plotted over time.

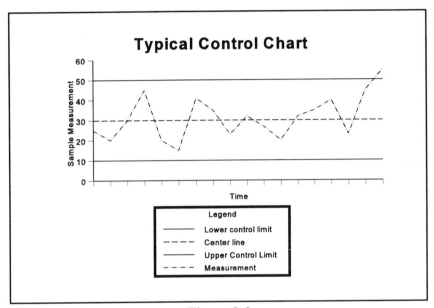

Figure 8-3

Measure stability over time

In the Control Chart above, you can graphically see the variability of the measurement charted over time. The upper and lower control limits are chosen so that if the process is in control, almost all sample points will be between these limits. For the charted process in Figure 8-3, all but the last data point are between the control limits.

As described below, the control limits are determined statistically based upon the inherent variability in the process. Process targets, specifications or budgets have no impact on the control limits.

Identify and remove assignable causes

As the last data point in the Control Chart was "out of control," it is more likely attributable to assignable causes and is a good choice for examination. Through analysis of the process at the point in time where the process was out of control, a determination can be made of the assignable cause of the variation. Once the *problem* is identified, the process can be altered or the cause isolated so that the problem does not reoccur.

Detect changes in the process

One type of control chart is called a **P Chart**. The P chart is used to monitor *fraction nonconforming data*.

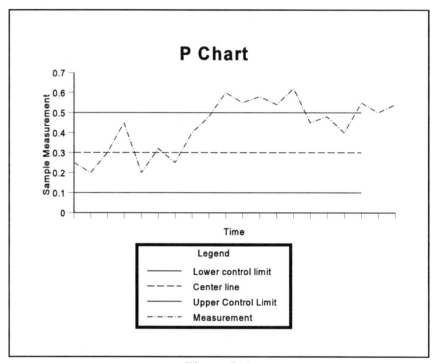

Figure 8-4

In Figure 8-4, a change in process performance is indicated at the point where the measurements increase. It is likely that there was an assignable cause or a change in the process creating this result.

When to use Control Charts

Control Charts can and should be used throughout all phases of a quality improvement program. Control Charts are one way in which a process "speaks" to you about how it is working. This graphical representation can be used to represent the state of a process before process improvement efforts begin, to discern whether a program is having effect, and to monitor the process to determine if changes have been successful. The earlier in a program SPC is introduced, the greater its effect.

There are five basic types of Control Charts. These charts can be classified by the type of data analyzed.

Attribute Data	Variables Data
P Chart- Fraction defective	$\bar{x}$ Chart - Average
C Chart - Defects	R Chart - Range
U Chart - Defects/unit	

Control Chart Basics

The center line for a Control Chart is, in theory, the value that the plotted variable should take if no assignable causes are present in the process. It is computed as the mean of the sample process data and the upper and lower control limits are located at three standard deviations of the variable plotted on the control chart from the center line. In this manner, nearly all of the chance variation in the process should be captured between the upper and lower control limits.

How the Control Chart Works

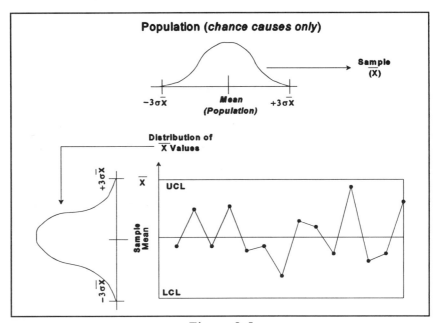

Figure 8-5

❶ The first step in creating a Control Chart is data gathering.

    ①   Determine the required sample size

    ②   Gather the data through random sampling from the process

❷ Calculate the chart parameters

    ①   Determine the sample mean for use as the center line of the Control Chart

    ②   Determine the sample standard deviation of the quantity to be plotted on the Control Chart. Multiply the standard deviation by 3 and -3 for use as the upper and lower control limits, respectively.

❸ Construct the chart

    ①   Determine the appropriate scale

    ②   Place the data measurement scale along the Y axis of the chart

    ③   On the X axis the time interval or sample number is indicated

    ④   Plot data on the chart

❹ Analyze the data

P Chart - Fraction Defective

The P Chart is also known as a fraction defective, proportion defective, or percentage nonconforming control chart because it is used to track data that is either conforming or nonconforming (defective). This type of data can be compared to a true/false or yes/no decision on each individual unit in the sample.

For P Charts the data is the number of nonconforming units divided by the sample size **n** to determine the fraction defective. For P Charts you generally take a series of samples over a period of time. Therefore each subgroup (sample for a particular time interval) would have its own percentage nonconforming.

$$\mathbf{p} = \text{number defective}/\mathbf{n}$$

The mean of the data would represent the average percentage nonconforming, or:

$$\bar{\mathbf{p}} = (\text{total \# defective})/(\text{total sample})$$
$$\sum \mathbf{p} \qquad / \quad \sum \mathbf{n}$$

The control limits are calculated by taking 3 times the standard deviation of p.

$$Control\ limits\ =\ \bar{p}\ \pm\ 3\sqrt{\frac{1\bar{p}(1-\bar{p})}{n}}$$

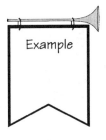

Example

You are in charge of a purchasing department which prepares approximately 250 purchase orders (P.O.) per week. In an effort to increase the quality of your product (P.O.s), you have instituted the use of Control Charts. Over the past 20 weeks you have randomly selected 25 P.O.s per week for analysis. The data is shown in Table 8-1.

The results are as follows:

Number of Purchase Orders Sampled	Number Requiring Rework	Week
25	1	1
25	2	2
25	1	3
25	0	4
25	3	5
25	1	6
25	2	7
25	0	8
25	2	9
25	5	10
25	1	11
25	2	12
25	0	13
25	1	14
25	8	15
25	1	16
25	2	17
25	1	18
25	3	19
25	5	20
500	41	

Table 8-1

Calculations for the P Chart are as follows:

Center line

$$\overline{P} = \frac{41}{500} = 0.082$$

Control limits

$$\overline{P} \pm 3 \frac{\sqrt{\overline{P} - (1 - \overline{P})}}{n}$$

$$0.082 \pm 3\sqrt{\frac{(0.082)\,(1-0.082)}{25}}$$

$$UCL = 0.082 + 0.165 = 0.247$$
$$LCL = 0.082 - 0.165 = -0.083 = 0$$

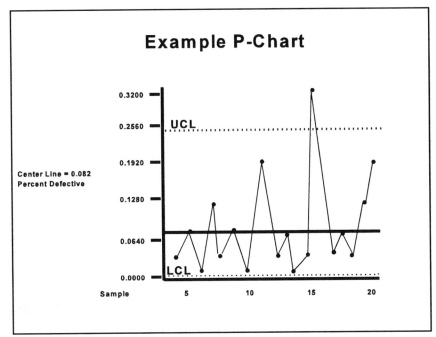

Figure 8-6 - Control Chart for Table 8-1

C Chart - Count Data

The C Chart is used to track attribute data representing a numerical count. It tracks the number of observed defects or errors rather than the fraction or proportion defective. For C Charts **c** = the number of defects on an item or document or in a service.

The center line (or mean) is calculated as:

$$CL = \overline{C} = \frac{Error\ Count}{Number\ of\ Observations}$$

The control limits are calculated as:

$$\overline{C} \pm 3\sqrt{\overline{C}}$$

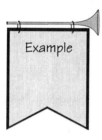

Example

Smith, Jones, and Brown, CPAs (SJB) is a local CPA firm preparing over 400 individual tax returns each year. Returns are prepared by staff accountants and then reviewed for accuracy and preferential tax treatment by one of the three partners. In the review process, a partner will write review notes which consist of instructions for the staff. These review notes are generally considered mistakes by the staff requiring rework. SJB has instituted a quality improvement program to reduce the errors on tax returns, increase productivity and reduce cost. One of the first steps taken was the tracking of tax return errors via the use of Control Charts. A sample of 24 returns was randomly selected. The data are shown on Table 8-2.

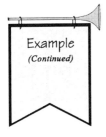

Example
(Continued)

Return Number	# of Review Notes
1	7
2	10
3	8
4	3
5	7
6	11
7	8
8	22
9	13
10	1
11	25
12	2
13	2
14	6
15	8
16	8
17	7
18	8
19	7
20	13
21	0
22	11
23	13
24	0
	200

Table 8-2

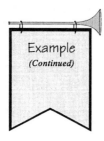

Example
(Continued)

$$\overline{C} = \frac{200}{24} = 8.3$$

$$UCL = \overline{C} + 3\sqrt{C} = 8.3 + 3\sqrt{8.3} \qquad LCL = \overline{C} - 3\sqrt{c} = 0$$

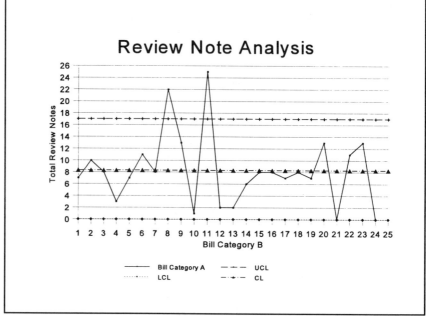

Figure 8-7 Control Chart for Table 8-2

U Charts - Defects per Unit

U Charts are used to track errors per inspection unit. Sometimes it is inconvenient to have homogeneous sample sizes over time. Other times inspection is 100% of all products or services resulting in unequal sample sizes. The U Chart allows the tracking of data when sample sizes vary from period to period or when an inspection unit is more than one. Another application of the U Chart occurs when defects have been classified under a weighing system. The U Chart can be used to combine the various errors into a composite score for tracking purposes. Calculations using the U Chart are as follows:

$$U = \text{defects per unit} = \frac{C}{n}$$

where c = errors or defects and n = number of items in sample

Center line = ū average of all u values

$$Control\ limits\ =\ \overline{u}\ \pm\ 3\sqrt{u/n}$$

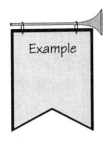

Example

WegetIt There, a local messenger service has developed a weighted service quality performance measurement system. Quality is considered getting the letter or package to the customer on or before the promised time. Demerits are assigned to different quality defects based upon level of severity. They are as follows:

Class A Defects - **Very serious** in nature that definitely decrease customer satisfaction and could potentially lose a customer. They include: lost, damaged or destroyed packages.

Class B Defects - **Serious** in nature that will cause customer dissatisfaction: They include: Delivering packages the day after due, and missed pick up.

Class C Defects - **Moderately serious** in nature that are likely to cause customer dissatisfaction but are common in the industry. They include: Late delivery or pick up on the specified day, not locating a package on request by the customer.

Class D Defects - **Minor** defects, unprofessional in appearance. They include: customers on hold longer than 5 minutes, customer complaints about messenger appearance, invoice adjustments, etc.

These defects were given weighing of:

$$A = 100 \qquad B = 50 \qquad C = 10 \qquad D = 1$$

Let C_A, C_B, C_C, and C_D represent the number of Class A, Class B, Class C and Class D defects, respectively in an inspection unit. Assume that WegetIt There uses a sample of 25 deliveries per selected day as an inspection unit. The aggregate number of demerits in an inspection unit is defined as:

$$D = 100C_A + 50C_B + 10C_C + 1C_D$$

WegetIt There has decided to select ten delivery days randomly per month to develop a montly score or service quality indicator (SQI). The number of demerits per unit is defined as:

$U = \dfrac{D}{10}$ Where D is the total number of demerits in all ten days.

SQI statistics were kept over a period of time and publicized. Each month the SQI was evaluated to determine the root cause of any score of $\bar{u} \geq 150$ (the initial UCL).

Interpreting Control Charts

Interpreting Control Charts can be more complicated than it appears. When first implementing an SPC system, assignable cause variation is likely to exist. Therefore, care must be taken in setting up a Control Chart.

In creating the first or trial Control Chart, you should attempt to develop control limits based upon an in-control process. When an assignable cause has been identified, the control limits are recalculated omitting the data point with the assignable cause. Out of control points due to non-random causes are eliminated from the calculation of control limits in order to base our future analysis on a process that is in control. As the assignable causes are removed from the calculations, the limits on the process become tighter and may cause additional parts to fall "out of control." These data points should be examined to determine if assignable causes are present.

As a process is brought into control over time, the control limits will need to be further adjusted to reflect the reduction in variability. There are some basic principles you can follow when interpreting Control Charts.

❶ Concentrate on data points that are outside of the control limits

❷ If a discernable change in pattern is noted, look for changes in the process.

❸ Patterns of seven or more points in an upward or downward trend, or seven points in sequence above or below the center line may indicate an assignable cause.

❹ A cyclical trend in data points may indicate seasonal effects.

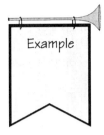

Example

A wholesaler of motorcycle parts has a stock of over 10,000 individual items. Each item has a unique item number designated by the company. The supplier also has its own item number which is stored in the inventory records. Sometimes, a single inventory item can have multiple suppliers. This situation has resulted in homogenous inventory items being assigned multiple inventory numbers which, in turn, has created confusion and errors in filling sales orders.

Customers have been told that parts are out of stock when, in fact, they are in; inventory counts have been incorrect; and cost of sales information has been incorrectly posted. Additionally, multiple vendors have received orders resulting in over stocking of inventory.

Through inspection of sales and inventory records, we can determine whether an order was properly placed and accounted for. The company is establishing a quality improvement program in which it plans to use statistical quality control principles. To establish a Control Chart, 30 samples of 50 orders were selected over a two week period.

Data for trial control limits, sample size $n = 50$

Sample Number	Number of Non-conforming Orders	Sample Fraction Nonconforming, p_i
1	12	0.24
2	15	0.30
3	8	0.16
4	10	0.20
5	4	0.08
6	7	0.14
7	16	0.32
8	9	0.18
9	14	0.28
10	10	0.20
11	5	0.10
12	6	0.12
13	17	0.34
14	12	0.24
15	22	0.44
16	8	0.16
17	10	0.20
18	5	0.10
19	13	0.26
20	11	0.22
21	20	0.40
22	18	0.36
23	24	0.48
24	15	0.30
25	9	0.18
26	12	0.24
27	7	0.14
28	13	0.26
29	9	0.18
30	6	0.12
	347	$p=0.2313$

Table 8-3

Example
(Continued)

Therefore control limits are calculated as:

$$UCL = \bar{p} + 3\sqrt{\frac{\bar{p}(1-\bar{p})}{n}} = 0.2313 + 0.1789 = 0.4102$$

and

$$LCL = \bar{p} - 3\sqrt{\frac{\bar{p}(1-\bar{p})}{n}} = 0.2313 - 0.1789 = 0.0524$$

The Control Chart with center line at $\bar{p}$ = 0.2313 and the above upper and lower control limits is shown in Figure 8-8. The sample fraction nonconforming from each preliminary samle is plotted on this chart. We note that two points, those from samples 15 and 23, plot above the upper control limit, so the process is not control. These points are investigated to determine whether an assignable cause can be determined.

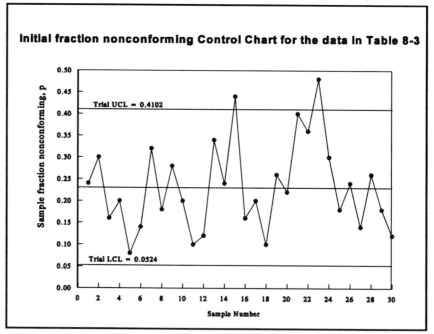

Figure 8-8

Example
(Continued)

Investigation of Sample 15 indicated that there was a network crash in which data was lost from all orders in-process at the time. It was not determined until later that data was lost and was subsequently recovered and corrected. Furthermore, during the period of time when Sample 23 was collected, a new temporary staff person was taking orders due to regular staff vacations. Consequently, Samples 15 and 23 are eliminated. The new center line and revised control limits are calculated as:

$$\overline{p} = \frac{301}{(28)50} = 0.2150$$

$$CL = \overline{p} \pm 3\sqrt{\frac{\overline{p}(1-\overline{p})}{n}} = 0.2150 \pm 3\sqrt{\frac{0.2150(0.7850)}{50}}$$

$$UCL = 0.3893, \qquad LCL = 0.0407$$

The revised center line and control limits are shown in Figure 8-9. Note that Samples 15 and 23 appear on the chart although they have been excluded from the calculations. The control chart has been annotated to indicate this change for documentation and future analysis purposes.

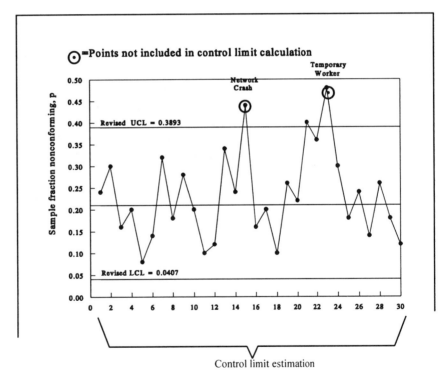

Figure 8-9 Revised Control limits for the data in Table 8-3

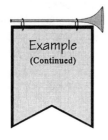

Example
(Continued)

Note that the point for Sample 21 now lies above the upper control limit. Preliminary analysis did not produce any identifiable assignable cause. In this case, the point will be retained in the calculations. The control limits will be accepted for future estimation of control.

Sometime further examination of Control Charts will uncover pattern changes or trends. In this example the largest run is 5 above the control line (Samples 19-24). If the temporary worker to whom the cause of point 23's variation was attributed, was working during samples 20-24, we would most likely discard all four samples even if points 21 and 23 exceeded the revised control limit.

The points would be inappropriate for inclusion on the grounds that the temporary worker probably has some adverse influence on the error rate throughout the time he/she worked.

When we conclude that the process is in control at the revised calculated levels, these limits are appropriate for further monitoring of the order taking/processing process. Although the process is "in control," the error rate is much too high. It is unlikely that the process quality can be improved by order takers trying harder, but that the process itself must be redesigned to improve performance.

In this example, it is obvious that the process of order entry and inventory management needs revision. A cross-functional task team is formed to analyze the process in an effort to reduce the systematic problems causing the high error rate. The team develops an action plan to refine the process. During the next three months, changes are made to the computer programs and order entry procedures. An additional 24 samples of 50 orders is collected during this time period. These data are shown in Table 8-4 and in Figure 8-10.

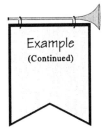

Example
(Continued)

Sample Number	Number of Nonconforming, D_i	Sample Fraction Nonconforming, p_i
31	9	0.18
32	6	0.12
33	12	0.24
34	5	0.10
35	6	0.12
36	4	0.08
37	6	0.12
38	3	0.06
39	7	0.14
40	6	0.12
41	2	0.04
42	4	0.08
43	3	0.06
44	6	0.12
45	5	0.10
46	4	0.08
47	8	0.16
48	5	0.10
49	6	0.12
50	7	0.14
51	5	0.10
52	6	0.12
53	3	0.10
54	5	0.10
	133	p=0.1108

Table 8-4

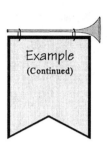

Example
(Continued)

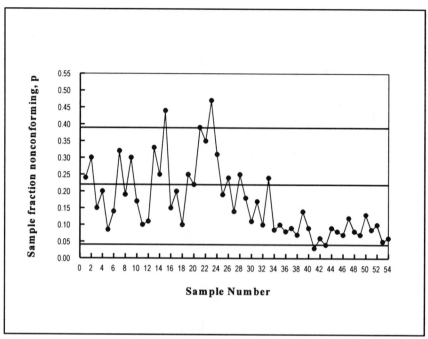

Figure 8-10 Continuation of P-Chart

Looking at Figure 8-10, an immediate impression is that the revised process is generating at an error rate well below the center line and sample 41 is even below the lower control limit. As no assignable cause is readily known for such peak performance, we can assume that the process performance criteria has changed significantly. The testing of this hypothesis can be performed using statistical methods.

Based upon the apparently successful process adjustments, the control limits are revised based upon the most recent sample data.

$$CL = \overline{p} = 0.1108$$

$$CL = \overline{p} \pm 3\sqrt{\frac{\overline{p}(1-\overline{p})}{n}} = 0.11.08 \pm 3\sqrt{\frac{(0.1108)(0.8892)}{50}} =$$

$$UCL = 0.2440 \qquad LCL = -0.0224 = 0$$

Figure 8-11 shows the Control Chart with these new parameters. Notice that the lower control limit has been set to zero (0) as you cannot have a negative error rate. Only points above the UCL will require inspection.

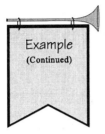

Example
(Continued)

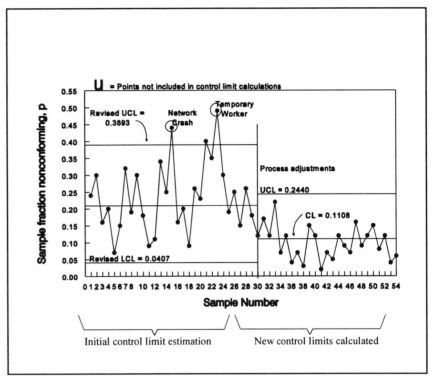

Figure 8-11

Although the process appears to be in control at the revised limits, an error rate of 11.08% is still too high. Further management action and/or continuance of the task team will be required to further correct the process.

Tips

✏ Control Charts are used to improve processes by identifying sources of variability and tracking process performance. These goals cannot be accomplished by applying Control Charts to a process at one point in time. The use of Control Charts is most applicable for continuous improvement of a process.

✏ SPC should be applied proactively, as a way to improve processes that are important to customers. SPC should not be used to apply blame to a person responsible for an assignable cause or the manager responsible for the process. Blame results in the manipulation of data and loss of confidence in a program.

✏   Control Charts need not be applied to every data measurement on every process. Apply SPC to key and leading indicators of performance. Take measurements at the critical control points in the process. Identify the earliest point in the process where an assignable cause has been identified and measure at that point.

✏   Integrate the SPC program into the process. If SPC is relegated to an after-the-fact analysis of data required by management it will not result in continuous improvement. Although by its nature SPC is performed after the errors have occurred, the closer to the activity the information is analyzed, the more impact it will have.

✏   Use small samples of data. Large samples or 100% sampling may not increase the effectiveness of the SPC program but will definitely add to the cost of quality.

✏   There are two potential fallacies in the interpretation of Control Charts.

①   Ascribing an error to an assignable cause when in fact the variation was inherent in the process.

This fallacy will result in overadjustment to the process. "Putting out fires is not improvement of the process." Treating every point that is out of control as an event that requires adjustment, and will result in so much adjustment that the process will not be stable enough to evaluate.

②   Ascribing an error to the process when the variation was assignable.

The action required to adjust a process is usually considerably greater than the elimination of an assignable cause. Special causes of variation should be identified and addressed immediately, while the occurrence is still fresh in everyone's mind. Systematic problems require an analysis of the effects of any process change.

Some analysts suggest using two sets of limits on Control Charts such as those shown in Figure 8-12. Instead of using the standard control limits, three standard deviations from the control line are the usual signal for the search for assignable causes, these analysts suggest using "warning lines" at two standard deviations. If one or more points fall in the "warning zone" between the two lines, additional investigation may be warranted. One potential "warning action" may be to increase the sampling frequency to increase the ability of the Control Chart to detect assignable causes more quickly.

Warning limits can potentially increase the sensitivity of the Control Chart. However, interpretation of the chart is not as definite, and staff creating the charts may attribute unwanted importance to its messages.

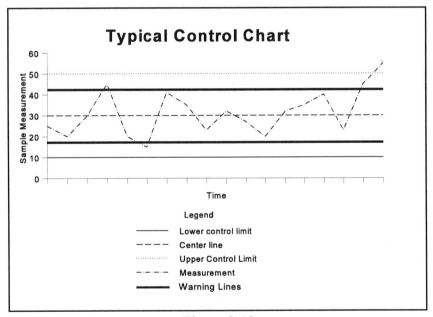

Figure 8-12

Outcome

Integration of SPC into your quality improvement program will improve the quality of decision making. As SPC is statistically based, information can be generated with a degree of certainty. SPC information is used to reduce variability in processes through the identification and removal of assignable causes.

Together with other quality improvement tools, Control Charts will help identify the root causes of problems so they can be eliminated. By implementing the use of Control Charts in a proactive manner, the cost of quality can be reduced and profitability increased.

Measurement Systems

Chapter Objectives

Measurement is an inseparable part of quality improvement and process redesign. Making decisive progress without knowing where you were, are, and want to be is nearly impossible.

This chapter provides an understanding of:

☞   Measurements Defined
☞   Why Measure?
☞   Measurement Systems
☞   What to Measure
☞   Types of Measurements
☞   How to Measure
☞   Where to Measure
☞   Cost of Quality

Measurements Defined

Measurements are the quantification of process attributes (functions or activities) that allow for the assessment of process performance. They are a systematic way of evaluating inputs, outputs, added value and productivity in a process.

A measurement system involves the collection and evaluation of data from key functions and indicators in a business process. These measures can be either **external measures** or **internal measures.**

External measures are from the viewpoint of the process customer and involve evaluating process output. Examples of external measures are customer satisfaction survey results and on-time delivery results.

Internal measures are used by the redesign team for analysis, planning, and problem solving. These measures cover a myriad of metrics, including cycle time, work-in-process backlog, subjective management evaluations and various output indicators.

Examples of measurements include:

- External

  ➢ Customer satisfaction
  ➢ Customer loyalty
  ➢ On-time delivery results
  ➢ Profit margin by product line

- Internal

  ➢ Timeliness
  ➢ Cost
  ➢ Efficiency
  ➢ Control

Both internal and external measurements may produce either **objective data** (i.e. time or money), requiring the use of numerical evaluations and assessment; or **subjective data** or **attribute data**, requiring measurement on a qualitative scale.

Why Measure?

The significance of measurements cannot be overemphasized. A measurement system provides the foundation for evaluating the current state of process performance, highlights the areas for improvement and establishes a means of continually evaluating and monitoring the performance of the business process.

- Measurement systems are integral regardless of whether the business process is undergoing gradual and incremental refinement or a radical redesign. Without an effective measurement system, there can be no way to confidently perform a successful improvement or redesign effort.

- Measurement systems allow management decision making to move away from being based on judgement and hunches formed without sufficient information. Decisions become more fact-based and objective.

- A measurement system also provides the information necessary to conduct analytical procedures on process attributes, including:

  ➤ Statistical Process Control (SPC)
  ➤ Benchmarking
  ➤ Quality Function Deployment

Measurement Systems

Measurements are useful only when evaluated and acted upon on a methodical basis. To facilitate this ongoing measurement and to ensure continuity over time, a **measurement system** must be incorporated into the business process. A measurement system is a systematic means of evaluating the inputs, outputs, added value and productivity in a process.

Attributes of an effective measurement system include the following:

❶ Allows for evaluation at a given point in time
❷ Allows for comparative evaluation over time
❸ Measurements are adequate to determine cause of changes
❹ Measurements must be distributed to, and evaluated by, those responsible for activity
❺ Measurements should not be used as a carrot or stick

❶ **Allows for evaluation at a given point in time**

Effective measurement systems allow for evaluation at a given point in time. They are a "snap shot" of process performance.

❷   **Allows for comparative evaluation over time**

Measurements must be evaluated over time in order to track progress and improvement. Take measurements on a regular, periodic interval to adequately identify trends and changes. Tools such as SPC help in this regard.

❸   **Measurements are adequate to determine cause of changes**

Measurements must be adequate to determine what causes change in measurements over time. Do changes reflect the quality of the process or are the changes due to other factors unrelated to quality?

❹   **Measurements must be distributed to, and evaluated by, those responsible for activity**

Measurement data must be distributed to, and evaluated by, the personnel who are responsible for the results and who can influence them. This ensures that any corrective actions taken are based on the correct data.

❺   **Measurements should not be used as a carrot or stick**

Measurement data should be used to evaluate trends for the processes of an organization, division or operation, and not for comparison between them. In a quality improvement or reengineering project, never use measurements as a carrot or a stick, but for process improvement purposes.

What to measure

Measurements are made of the key functions or indicators in a process. Measurements should be taken and evaluated within the following five categories:

❶   Quality
❷   Productivity
❸   Timeliness
❹   Cost
❺   Culture

---

❶   Quality

This category includes measurable attributes in the context of customer expectations, product specifications and actual results.

❷   Productivity

Productivity is a measure of the utilization of resources and the efficiency of a process. It is a comparison of resources consumed and ultimate process output.

❸   Timeliness

This is the ability of a process to meet time deadlines and expectations, both those imposed by external and internal customers.

❹   Cost

Cost is the gross amount of resources used in a process. The amount of product or services produced in a process is usually not considered in determining cost.

❺   Culture

These are the behavioral characteristics inherent in a process or organization. Culture includes the amount of effort and time devoted to process improvement and the morale of the process participants.

These five process categories influence process performance, whether evaluated externally (by process customers) or internally. They are the primary determinates of process efficiency and the ultimate success of the organization.

However, measurement and evaluation of these relatively broad process characteristics require closer analysis of the specific activities within a process. The performance of the detailed activities within a process influence the performance of the entire process and are therefore measured and evaluated.

Types of Measurements

A basic measurement system includes the following measurements:

- **Work product or units produced** - What are the physical items that are handled within the process? (Examples: proposals, PO's, checks, money, requests, engineering plans, etc.)

- **Resources consumed** - Look at the particular resources that the business process uses. (Examples: people, money, equipment). Measurements often focus on the rate or quantity of resources utilized.

- **Value added** - Focus on the value added by the business activity or process. What functions within the process add value to the product or services generated?

The following four assessment categories should be used to gather and evaluate measurements:

❶ Output/Raw Data
❷ Subjective Rating
❸ Indicators/Ratios
❹ Behavioral Measures

❶ **Output/Raw Data**

This represents data such as frequency counts and other data that can be compared to goals and budgets. This is the least involved measurement procedure since a simple comparison to a benchmark is the only analytical requirement.

Types of data:

- Number of customer complaints
- Times a document is late
- Glitches in a computer program
- Overtime hours worked
- Equipment use time

❷ **Subjective Rating**

This involves the subjective scoring of satisfaction or opinion on a numerical scale. This procedure is more art than science since opinion varies among those being surveyed.

Types of data:

- Performance rankings
- Customer satisfaction surveys
- Customer suggestions
- Job performance evaluations

❸ **Indicators/Ratios**

Indicators and ratios reflect process efficiency, timeliness, or use of resources. Such information is useful in establishing trends and measures of performance.

Types of data:

- Speed with which orders are processed
- Response time to change orders
- Number of items released on time versus total
- Number of items released for production
- Variances

❹ **Behavioral Measures**

This quantifies the behavior patterns of people by measuring attitude, perspective, and time spent on problem solving and other process improvement efforts. This metric bears directly on the success of the team in making redesign work and is largely governed by management commitment to improvement and redesign.

Types of data:

- Time devoted to quality improvement meetings
- Employee morale surveys
- Time devoted to training

Table 9-1 reflects the types of measurements generally utilized within each of the measurement categories. These measures are usually attainable in most organizations and can be gathered with reasonable effort.

Measurement Evaluation					
	Quality	**Productivity**	**Timeliness**	**Cost**	**Culture**
Output/Raw Data	Number of complaints Number of suggestions Number of improvements Number of rejections	Profit $ Hours worked	Order processing speed Response time	Labor cost Capital expenditures	Number of recognitions Number of Q&A meetings
Subjective Rating	Rating systems for customer complaints Rating systems for customer suggestions Evaluation by knowledgeable experts	Management evaluation of progress toward goals Team evaluation of progress toward goals	Customer satisfaction ratings	Management evaluation Team rankings of opportunities for efficiencies	Employee satisfaction ratings Upward evaluations Job performance evaluations
Indicators/ Ratios	Number of defects/output Rework/output Rejection rate Response time	Project margin % Output/Input Financial variances Capacity utilization	# On schedule/total output Cycle time Turnaround time	Cost vs. budget Resources used/available NPV	%Projects on culture vs. process
Behavioral Measures	Time spent on problem solving Time spent on training Amount of customer contact	Time spent on problem solving	Time spent on process redesign Time spent on problem solving	Time spent on process redesign Time spent on problem solving	Time spent on process redesign Time spent on problem solving

Table 9-1

How to Measure

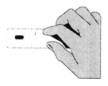

Most measurements are made from taking a *sample* of data from the business process. This allows the team to gather reliable data based on information representative of the entire population of data present within the process.

At the outset, it is common to gather and analyze 100% of the data. This is the natural tendency, especially during Process Activity Analysis and during the other fact gathering stages conducted early in the redesign process. However, the gathering of this amount of information is rarely necessary and should be discouraged. You should strive toward the use of **sample data** because:

• samples require less time and money to gather; and

• the data gathered via samples can usually be as reliable as using 100% of the data population if sampling is done correctly.

Where to Measure

Measurements should ideally be taken early in the business process in order to promote <u>prevention</u>. This allows elimination of the source/root cause of the defect or other inhibitor at the earliest possible point, before it can lead to other defects and errors.

Measurements are made of the key functions and activities of a process, usually referred to as the key indicators. Key indicators typically occur at the interface between the process and its supplier(s) or customer(s). Thus, measurements should be taken on key indicators as early in the process as possible.

Hazard Analysis and Critical Control Point Analysis (HA/CCP)

HA/CCP is a technique used to determine the appropriate place within a process to implement a measurement system. It effectively ties the results of Process Activity Analysis (PAA) together with the measurement system. Additionally, it serves to obtain measurements of key and leading indicators as early in the process as possible.

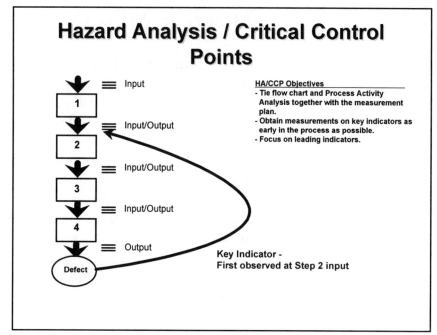

Figure 9-1

The process map or flowchart generated from PAA which includes all inputs and outputs at each step of the process is used to identify CCPs. The final output (product or service) of the process is evaluated to determine the key indicators of process quality and performance, and the characteristics of the output that add value to the customer.

The process map or flowchart is then analyzed to determine the earliest point in the process at which the particular key indicator can be observed. Ask the question, "Where in the process do we begin to add that particular key indicator to the product or service?" That point becomes a CCP, a place where a measurement is taken.

The challenge to this technique is that very quickly there will be far too many CCPs at which you can reasonably implement measurement systems. If this occurs, a management decision must be made as to which CCPs to focus attention and where to maintain measurement points.

You should avoid taking all measurement at the end of the process, where it interfaces with the ultimate customer. At that point, it is usually too late to avoid errors or problems since all the costs involved in producing the goods or service have been incurred. Additional cost must be incurred to ready the product to meet the customer's needs.

Cost of Quality

It is typically helpful to analyze process performance and to plan improvement efforts in terms of the **Cost of Quality**. This notion is that all products or services have some quality characteristics which carry a cost to achieve. It requires organizational resources to incorporate quality attributes into a product or service.

Components of Cost of Quality include:

❶　　Prevention
❷　　Appraisal
❸　　Internal failure
❹　　External failure

❶　Prevention

The resources devoted to preventing defects and failure. Examples include:

- Quality training
- Quality engineering
- Pilot studies

❷　Appraisal

Resources used for inspection of the work product. Examples include:

- Component testing
- Test of raw materials
- Reliability testing

❸   **Internal failure**

Resources consumed in correcting failure within the
process (rework). Examples include:

- Cost of scrap
- Cost of disposal
- Rework, labor and overhead

❹   **External failure**

Cost associated with problems discovered by the process
customer that affects them negatively or creates rework and
reprocessing. Examples include:

- Cost of responding to customer complaints
- Product recalls
- Warranty repairs and replacements

It is common for the Cost of Quality to run as high as 20% to 25%
of total revenue. Research has shown that as the investment in
prevention increases, the total cost of quality decreases. Thus,
emphasis should be placed on the resources devoted to the
prevention stage. Our experience suggests that the overall Cost of
Quality can be significantly reduced when the prevention
investment represents approximately 40% to 50% of the Cost of
Quality. Figure 9-2 reflects this relationship. The objective is to
reduce the cost associated with the remaining three categories of
Cost of Quality.

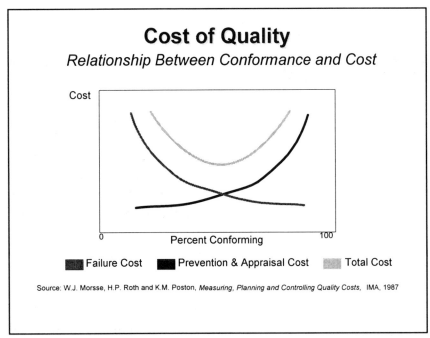

Figure 9-2

Cost of Quality should be analyzed as follows:

- The data gathered need not be as precise as typical accounting data, but only accurate enough to determine the order of magnitude. Do not view this data as financial accounting information.

- The costs should be used to identify problems and areas of opportunity.

- Quality cost data should be effectively communicated to those in the organization or process that can take corrective action.

- Quality costs should be tracked over time. If the business process is undergoing successful improvement or redesign, the cost of quality should go down over time.

Tips

✏ **Insufficient "Process" Orientation**

Often, those that manage business processes do not view them as a process, but as an activity or series of activities that are unrepeatable. They often believe "things" can be measured but processes cannot. Process Activity Analysis, if approached correctly, should force those responsible for business activities to view them as a process. This greatly facilitates the establishment of a measurement system.

✏ **Fear**

Additionally, there is a certain fear among those responsible for a business process that management will use measurement results for personnel evaluation instead of as an indicator of process performance. This misuse of process measurements inhibits the use and value of measurements as a means to improve the process. This is a cultural issue and the result is often that the goal becomes to manipulate the data for self preservation.

✏ **Overemphasis on Accuracy**

Too much emphasis has been placed on the accuracy of measurements themselves. The emphasis should be on gathering information that is of the correct magnitude and is timely. The information generated by the measurement system need not be of financial accounting quality but should be of a scale that is useful for management purposes. This point cannot be overemphasized in that many quality improvement and reengineering projects have failed and have been judged unsuccessful because an overemphasis on accuracy of measurement data resulted in a loss of focus and momentum. Do not sacrifice timeliness in order to achieve greater accuracy in measurement data.

✏ **Measuring Too Much**

Closely related to the overemphasis on measurement accuracy is the problem of measuring too much. As will be seen early in Process Activity Analysis, there are many sources of measurement data. To attempt to take too many measurements dilutes the effort and can create a loss of momentum.

✏ **Measuring the Wrong Things**

There is a natural motivation to measure in areas where you already excel. This is counter-productive to an improvement project and can reduce the effort to a publicity campaign. The goal is to identify and improve areas and activities where you do not currently excel.

✏ **Appropriate Data for Benchmarking**

If benchmarking is to be conducted, it is important that the measurement data be such that it can be readily compared to other similar processes, organizations and industries. The data must appropriately weigh the most important factors and process indicators and must reveal the most about the effectiveness of the process.

✏ **Customer Orientation**

As in all aspects of process improvement and reengineering, it is imperative that the measurement system identify how the process customers measure process effectiveness. This customer orientation must be incorporated into the measurement plan.

CHAPTER 10

Benchmarking

Chapter Objectives

At its core, benchmarking is learning from others. American advertisers used to joke at how the Japanese disassembled American products to learn how they were made. This was an early form of benchmarking. Today, benchmarking is one of the most common process improvement initiatives.

Many companies have had limited success with reengineering and process improvement and view benchmarking as the means to break old paradigms and achieve quantum leaps in performance. Other companies begin process improvement by benchmarking against industry leaders. The use of benchmarking has been driven by the Malcolm Baldrige Award. Section 2.2 of the 1995 award criteria specifically asks for "information on how competitive comparisons and benchmarking information are selected and used to drive improvement of overall company performance."

This chapter provides an introduction to benchmarking and insight into effective benchmarking. Chapter objectives include:

- ☞ Provide an overview of the benchmarking process
- ☞ Inform regarding benchmarking ethics
- ☞ Furnish steps for effective benchmarking
- ☞ Convey the importance of advance preparation
- ☞ Provide tools to aid in the benchmarking process

Concepts

In benchmarking, one or more companies that are "world class" in performing a specific process are sought out to learn *how* they achieve their performance level. A classic example of benchmarking is from Xerox, one of the pioneers in American benchmarking. When Xerox sought to improve order fulfillment it chose L.L. Bean as its benchmarking partner. Although copiers and outdoor gear have little in common, the process of picking and shipping parts varying in size and shape is essentially the same.

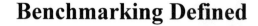

Benchmarking Defined

A benchmark is defined as a measurement used as a point of reference. However, benchmarking is not merely the act of taking a measurement. To be effective, the measurement must be linked to the methods or drivers of process performance. Therefore, benchmarking strives to answer the questions:

> *What are the measures of performance?*
> *What are the performance measures of the best performers?*
> *How do the best performers achieve their high marks?*

Therefore, we define benchmarking as:

> **The process of measuring and comparing a company's performance against that of another to improve its own performance**.

Three distinct types of benchmarking are **strategic, performance** and **process**.

- **Strategic benchmarking** is used to identify and emulate business strategies that enable other organizations to succeed. Examples of strategic benchmarking include:

  ➢ Product and service selection strategies; and
  ➢ Goal setting strategies for product performance, customer service, asset usage, financial ratios, etc.

  Strategic benchmarking results in long-term improvement in profitability and competitiveness.

- **Performance benchmarking** is utilized for comparing performance characteristics such as price, cost, product features or quality. Performance benchmarking focuses on outcomes as opposed to methods. Performance benchmarking assists in determining the product or service attributes that lead to customer satisfaction and the vital performance measures that guide an organization.

• **Process benchmarking** is a method for determining the best practices for a particular process regardless of industry. Process benchmarking focuses on work systems, functions and activities. Process benchmarking is utilized to obtain rapid improvement in process efficiency and profitability.

Process benchmarking is the most commonly utilized form and is the focus of this chapter.

As depicted in Figure 10-1, the business planning pyramid begins with a corporate vision and proceeds through the design or redesign of business processes. Benchmarking can assist in establishing each of these fundamental building blocks for organizational excellence. The business process results in performance indicators, which facilitate the evaluation of whether the strategy, and therefore the vision, are attainable. This chapter focuses on process benchmarking as the foundation for achieving dramatic process improvement.

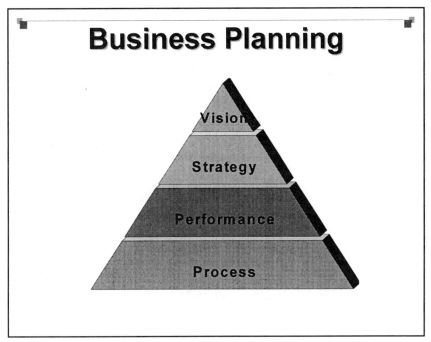

Figure 10-1

Benchmarking Methods

Benchmarking is performed by individuals following a multi-step process to compare current activities against those of another group or entity. The benchmarking process may be a **formal** process, as described in this chapter, or it may be **informal**.

Informal benchmarking is an unstructured approach to learning from others. Informal benchmarking includes:

- Learning from past experiences
- Learning from associated entities or other departments within an organization
- Reading about other companies' success stories
- Conversing with individuals at conferences and professional society meetings

These actions become benchmarking when that information is compared to your own organization's practices.

Informal benchmarking is inexpensive and can produce tangible results. However, informal benchmarking does not typically produce the same depth of understanding that results from a formalized, team-based effort.

We recommend establishing a formal benchmarking program with which to improve performance when redesigning core processes, or processes with large opportunities for improvement. Informal benchmarking is more appropriate for support or subprocesses when utilizing an incremental approach to process improvement.

What to benchmark

Many organizations choose processes to benchmark based upon customer feedback, budget overruns or high error rates. This approach to selecting benchmarks can be described as problem-based benchmarking. While this approach may alleviate frustrations and improve performance, it may not be the appropriate method for selecting the best processes to benchmark.

The Pareto principle states that 80% of value comes from 20% of activities. Therefore, 80% of the activities may not be worthy of benchmarking. The remaining 20% includes the key processes of a business. As discussed throughout this text, core business processes hold the greatest opportunity for improvement, and should therefore be the main focus of formal benchmarking.

As formal benchmarking is not simple or inexpensive, an analysis of cost and benefit is required. The analysis should:

- evaluate key processes to determine which have the greatest impact on customer satisfaction and/or profitability;

- determine which key processes have the largest gap between desired or demanded performance and actual performance; and

- convert the information gathered into a dollar estimate of potential savings or increased revenue.

This analysis should facilitate a reliable decision on which processes to benchmark.

When to benchmark

For benchmarking to succeed, a company must have a clear focus on the goals and objectives of the benchmarking process. To have a clear focus, the company must know the current condition of its processes and how that status influences performance. Accordingly, benchmarking is generally for companies in a mature state of process management.

Requisite knowledge for undertaking benchmarking includes:
- Identification of customers
- Understanding of customer requirements
- Identification of core business processes
- Definition and understanding of core processes
- Baseline measurements of performance

Methods for obtaining this requisite data are discussed throughout this text.

The Benchmarking Process

The benchmarking process should be directly linked to the overall process improvement effort. It should be driven by the vision, mission and strategic plan of the organization, built on a foundation of measurement and aimed at the root cause of process efficiency or inefficiency. To ensure the endeavor does not undermine other efforts, benchmarking should be coordinated within the scope of the overall process improvement program.

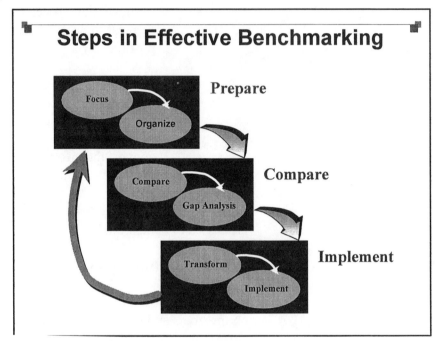

Steps in Effective Benchmarking

Prepare — Focus, Organize

Compare — Compare, Gap Analysis

Implement — Transform, Implement

Figure 10-2

Preparation Phase

Prior to engaging in a benchmarking study, the company should focus and organize its efforts. The preparation phase consists of planning and design activities required to ensure effective comparison and implementation phases.

The preparation phase consists of five activities:

    ❶   Steering Committee Commitment
    ❷   Opportunity Identification
    ❸   Risk Benefit Assessment
    ❹   Recommend Actions
    ❺   Work Plan and Schedule

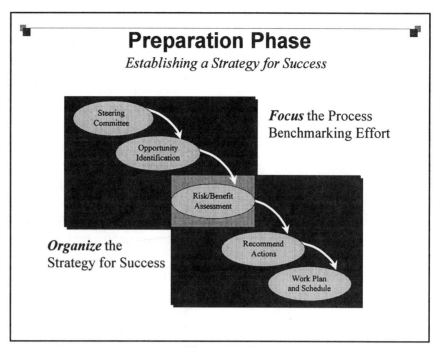

Preparation Phase

Establishing a Strategy for Success

Focus the Process Benchmarking Effort

Organize the Strategy for Success

Figure 10-3

❶ **Steering Committee Commitment** - The commitment of executive leadership is critical to ensure the allocation of adequate resources, time and funding for the benchmarking project. Without an executive sponsor and endorsement from the process improvement steering committee, the likelihood of project success is diminished. Sponsorship by, and communication with, the steering committee will ensure that the benchmarking effort is coordinated with the overall improvement program.

The effort must also be in congruence with the company's vision, mission and strategic plan. Prior to embarking on the formal benchmarking effort, the applicable business processes should be identified and linked to the organization's mission and goals. This foundation of knowledge can then be used by the steering committee to prioritize potential benchmarking projects.

Once the target process is known, the steering committee should charter an appropriate team to continue the process. Included on this team should be the process owner and others with a vested interest in the performance of that process.

❷ **Opportunity Identification** - What processes or attributes should the company benchmark? Usually the steering committee or senior management sponsors an effort to evaluate a process or a broad grouping of activities. In the opportunity identification step, the benchmarking team identifies the specific activities to benchmark.

The process model and measurements established by the primary process management program are used to determine specific key processes and subprocesses possessing the greatest benchmarking potential. The Process Selection Matrix (Figure 3-7) discussed in Chapter 3 can be useful to determine which processes have the greatest impact on business objectives and therefore are the best candidates for benchmarking.

Based upon the current state of performance, a benchmarking team can determine where the greatest opportunities lie. The Process Rating System (Exhibit A) and Process Performance Profile (Table 10-1) are useful tools to evaluate current process performance.

Another method for determining which processes to benchmark is performance benchmarking. As discussed earlier in this chapter, comparing your performance with that of your competition may indicate specific areas of need.

Whether derived through performance benchmarking or an informal analysis, an estimate of the optimal performance measure or measures should be determined. For instance, these measures could be anticipated customer satisfaction measurement based upon industry data, estimated throughput time for a process, or a revised product cost. Performance estimates are required to determine the potential benefit of the effort.

Process Performance Profile

Process Name _____ Process Owner _____

Process Output:

Process Customer:

Process Performance Measures:	Current Level	Trend

		Current Level	Trend
Quality	Conformance Rate	_____	_____
	Customer returns	_____	_____
	Rework rate	_____	_____
Cost	Process cost	_____	_____
	Process value-added	_____	_____
	Value-to-cost ratio	_____	_____
Cycle	Process cycle time	_____	_____
Time	Process walk-through time	_____	_____
	Process downtime	_____	_____

Process Performance Goals:	Short-term	Long-term
Conformance Rate	_____	_____
Value-to-cost ratio	_____	_____
Cycle time	_____	_____

Table 10-1

❸ **Risk Benefit Assessment** - For each opportunity there is a risk, and for every benefit there will be a cost. The risk/benefit assessment stage prioritizes efforts to achieve the greatest results with the least resources.

Risks and benefits can be measured in terms of dollars, culture or time. For example, proceeding with a benchmarking effort involving a department that is resistant to change will take an expenditure of political capital. That may cost the company in terms of time spent influencing the resistant manager, and dollars to generate data sufficient to break the resistance.

---

❹ **Recommend Actions** - The benchmarking team recommends an action plan to the steering committee. The plan include estimates of:

    ① Time commitment
    ② Cost
    ③ Revenue and/or proficiency enhancement

Although the detail work of the comparison phase has not yet been completed, cost estimates can be made based upon similar projects, or obtained from consultants or other sources. For example, a benchmarking project for a well-defined subprocess in a medium sized organization may require a team of three individuals for a six month period investing 25% of their total time on the project. A large benchmarking project for a less well-defined process in a large organization may require a full-time 6-8 member team for over one year.

The steering committee will then endorse the plan and ensure that the required resources are provided. Without endorsement and an allocation of resources, the benchmarking effort will suffer a tenuous existence with less chance of breakthrough results.

❺ **Work Plan and Schedule** - Once the project has been approved, the benchmarking team develops a detailed work plan and project time line. The work plan is evaluated periodically during the project through comparison with monthly progress reports.

Comparison Phase

During the comparison phase the benchmarking team analyzes one or more benchmarking partner's performance to discover the best practices. The comparison phase consists of five activities:

    ❶ Selecting Benchmarking Partner(s)
    ❷ Analyzing Partner Performance
    ❸ Determining Performance Gaps
    ❹ Determining Root Cause of Gaps
    ❺ Modifying Best Practice for the Environment

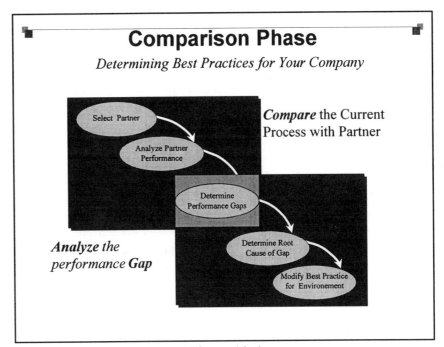

Figure 10-4

❶   **Selecting Benchmarking Partner(s)** - Selecting benchmarking partners can be one of the most difficult tasks, especially for a company in its first benchmarking effort.

Based upon the knowledge gained from the internal process evaluation, the benchmarking team must determine the characteristics of a potential partner. Searching for external partners can be facilitated through benchmarking consortiums and information networks such as "The Benchmarking Exchange" or "Benchmarking Clearinghouse." Other sources may be suppliers, major customers, industry associations and external consultants who have a distinguished client base.

The partner may not necessarily be external to the company. The partner can be another department, division or unit of the company. The key to selecting a partner is determining that the target's performance is superior to the process being studied.

Researching partners

Once a short list of potential partners is developed, research into each of the company's operating environments is required. Factors such as corporate culture, ownership and organizational structure, and industry characteristics influence the transferability of company practices.

A variety of information can and should be obtained through publicly available information. Sources such as Dun and Bradstreet, Value Line, CompuServe, professional societies, industry publications, governmental studies and external consultant surveys can provide valuable information for identifying a partner. Additionally, this public information serves as the backbone of the initial contact questionnaire with the potential partner.

A preliminary comparison of performance criteria is summarized. Table 10-2 is an excerpt from a form used for an information systems department benchmarking study.

Partner Profile & Environment	Company Name		

Business size
  # employees
  Sales revenue			

Industry classification Principal product/service			
Organizational structure			

Company culture
  Formality
  Management style			

# of Workstations			
Hardware			
I/S department size			
etc.			

Table 10-2

The initial comparison of available external data with your own performance measures often leads to insight for process improvement.

Once the external data gathering is complete you are ready to propose benchmarking partners to the steering committee. The benchmarking team should be prepared to answer the following questions:

- Are we sure that these companies have superior performance?
- Is the data collected recent and reliable?
- Is the information comparable, or are there too many industry or environmental differences to warrant partnering?
- Will the potential partner be willing to directly share information?

These questions should be answered based upon the study performed. If not, more research is warranted.

Once you have selected potential partners, you must contact the appropriate person at the target firm and present your effort to get agreement to perform the study. Contacting the wrong manager or not positioning the study as mutually beneficial may result in rejection.

The better prepared both partners are for the site visit, the more efficient and productive the benchmarking effort will be

Partnering with another organization requires the sharing of information and willingness to reciprocate with access to your facilities. Do not ask for something that you are not willing to provide to your partner. Discuss the specificity of information desired and the documentation methods used. The better prepared both partners are for the site visit, the more efficient and productive the benchmarking effort will be.

Prior to visiting the partner site, logistical details, confidentiality agreements and other conduct guidelines must be negotiated. Ethical and conduct considerations are discussed later in this chapter.

Tips

✐ The cost and time required for benchmarking increases with the number of partners selected. The benefits of the study also increase as the number of benchmarking partners increase. There is no consensus on the specific number of companies with which to partner for a formal benchmarking effort, but most experts agree that for key processes, three to six partners may be appropriate.

✐ When looking for partners, "superior performance" can be classified in varying ways. Superior performance should not be defined as "better than us." In ascending order, superior performance should be considered:

- Best in company
- Industry standard
- Industry leader
- Best in class (process)
- World class

Due to financial constraints you may be limited to a category such as "best in region." Do not waste your time or money on a formal benchmarking project for just "better than us."

❷ **Analyzing Partner Performance** - Advance preparation is crucial for productive site visits and the building of an ongoing benchmarking relationship. Prior to the visit the benchmarking team should:

- Verify the accuracy of research performed prior to the visit;
- Ensure that all team members are aware of the partner's corporate culture, including degree of:
  - ➤ Formality
  - ➤ Empowerment;
- Communicate major objectives and activities of the visit; and
- Prepare and forward a specific benchmarking questionnaire.

The benchmarking questionnaire

The benchmarking questionnaire becomes the focal point for the initial contact between partners. To qualify partnering requests, some companies ask for a sample questionnaire to determine preparedness and maturity of the potential partner's process improvement effort.

If possible, test the questionnaire in a real world situation. For larger companies, the questionnaire can be tested with another division or location. The test should ensure that the questions:

- Are not ambiguous;
- Can be answered in a reasonable period of time;
- Promote discussion and learning; and
- Are directed toward the objectives of the visit.

The questionnaire will serve as the road map during the visit and will set the tone for the meetings. Questions should progress from general to more specific. General questions lead to open discussion and familiarity. Asking specific questions initially may increase defensiveness before a rapport and comfort level have been established.

Contents of the questionnaire should be aimed at determining:

- How the partner defines the process;
- Process measurement techniques;
- Performance measures and goals;
- Process problems and improvements; and
- Process enablers.

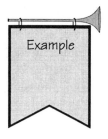

Example

Money First Bank created a benchmarking team to learn how companies change culture from one of entitlement to empowerment. The benchmarking team chose a national insurance company and a local manufacturing concern as benchmarking partners. Both companies had undergone successful culture change programs.

The bank had defined the problem as a people issue. One team member, an executive vice president at the bank, was quoted as saying, "if the people weren't so fat and happy with their 9-5 jobs and took some pride in their work, we wouldn't need this project." The two benchmarking partners had defined the process in terms of leadership (i.e. if people are led and well managed, they will take stewardship of their responsibilities).

Without altering the definition of the problem, the bank could not apply the methodologies employed by the partners.

Process enablers are the practices at the root cause of process efficiency. If a change in management style is the technique to be employed by the bank, a process enabler for that change might be leadership training and coaching.

Data Gathering

Information gathering must be performed in an organized fashion to facilitate comparison and analysis. Data gathering encompasses:

❶ Determining the key performance measures
❷ Determining how, where, when and by whom the data will be collected
❸ Determining the required data precision
❹ Collecting and validating the data

Determination of key performance measures is one of the most critical components of data gathering. You can expertly gather irrelevant information without producing any benefit. Therefore, it is crucial to discuss key performance indicators with partners prior to comparing information.

At the initial meetings, you should give information to the partner about your understanding of the process, its objectives and key performance indicators. This base knowledge provides the partner with the ability to point out any fundamental differences in their view of the process. These differences must be normalized for accurate data comparison.

Realize that the initial visit will include a bonding process, where you and your partner will be getting to know one another. Initial information exchanges may be strategic and general in nature. Once relationships have been established and both organizations recognize the benefits of the benchmarking study, the data exchanged and level of effort expended will become more specific.

Prepare documentation guidelines prior to the visit. Documentation guidelines:

- Ensure comparability among staff; and
- Provide structure to data gathering.

In addition, future reference by other internal benchmarking teams will be facilitated by a common methodology. Data can be summarized in a form similar to Table 10-3 to facilitate easy comparison of key ratios and indicators.

Performance Measure	Company Name		
Development costs (%)			
Support costs (%)			
Enhancement costs (%)			
Technicians per workstation			
Training $ per programer			
Customer satisfaction rating			
Turnaround / change order			
etc.			

Table 10-3

Tips

➥ If you are embarking on your first benchmarking project, consider the purchase and modification of existing benchmarking questionnaires. Questionnaires that have been tested are available through benchmarking consortiums and consulting firms. Care must be taken to tailor the questions to the specific objectives of your company.

➥ As more companies become involved in benchmarking, software vendors have begun developing application packages specifically designed to aid in the benchmarking process. Some packages provide a standard work plan and methodology that can be tailored to almost any project. In addition, software packages are useful for organizing data gathered.

❸ **Determining Performance Gaps**

Once the key drivers of performance have been established and partner measures have been gathered, you are ready to compare performance.

Data must be similar for comparison. The two keys to data comparison are *normalization* and *stratification*.

Normalization

Normalization refers to adjusting for differences in measurement techniques. It is quite common for companies to have different classifications for the costs of similar activities. For example, is the cost of developing a custom reporting module for an existing program an enhancement or a development cost?

Companies may use different methods of data collection. Company A may use a small judgmental sample to gather the information on its processes, while Company B utilizes statistical sampling with a 95% confidence level. Comparing the two measures without considering the impact of the sampling methods may lead to the erroneous conclusion that Company A's process was better, even though its sample was biased.

Stratification

Data should be stratified to aid in comparison. Stratification is the segregation into like groups. It is clear that smaller groups of information are easier to analyze. Data stratification can assist in:

- Identifying causes of variation;
- Identifying correlation among trends in data; and
- Selecting transactions for observation when additional data is required.

One useful tool for data stratification is the cause and effect diagram (see Chapter 7). The head of the diagram can represent the type of transaction and the skeleton can represent the major classifications of transactions. Conversely, the head can represent the critical performance measure, while the skeleton represents factors that influence the measure. In this manner the cause and effect diagram can be used to show relationships among the various measurements. Another useful tool for showing the relationships among performance measures is the force field diagram.

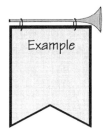

Example

Bob's Construction decided to benchmark the process of project management. It performed research and selected Iman Engineering Company and Debig Contractors Inc. as their benchmarking partners.

On the surface, Iman's performance seemed quite erratic when taken as a whole, while Debig's performance measures appeared superior.

Further analysis indicated that Iman's projects vary in length and complexity as opposed to Debig's, which are all large but simple. When Iman's large and simple projects are segregated from their smaller and more complex ones, their project management process proved to be far superior to Debig's.

Identifying Performance Gaps

After creating comparable data through normalization and stratification, the data can be evaluated in various ways to identify performance gaps. We recommend beginning your analysis by completing Table 10-3 with revised information and an additional column for "best of benchmark."

The information can then be presented graphically with bar charts or a **radar diagram**. A radar diagram depicts the goal for the specific key performance measures on the outside of the circle and the current performance (dark line) and best of benchmark (white line) as rings within the circle. As illustrated in Figure 10-5, the data measures have been converted to a percentage of the goal for comparability.

In Figure 10-5, the organization was best in class in Measure 2, competitive in Measures 1 and 4, but lagged behind in Measures 3 and 5.

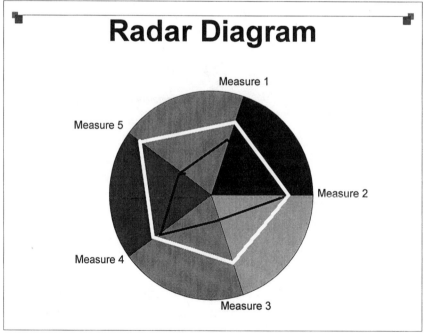

Figure 10-5

❹   **Determining Root Cause of Gaps**

Simply identifying the gaps is not sufficient for improving
the quality of the process. The root causes of the measured
gaps must be identified *and* analyzed.

In Figure 10-5 the company appears relatively strong in
three of the five performance indicators. Does this analysis
indicate that performance improvement in the two lagging
indicators will lead to enhanced efficiency? At this point
you may ask the questions:

- How do the performance indicators affect
  profitability?
- What is the relative importance of the
  individual performance measures to overall
  process performance?
- How does one performance measure affect
  other performance measures?

Regression Analysis

Regression analysis is a statistical technique for modeling
and investigating the relationship between two or more
variables. Regression analysis is one of the most common
methods for analyzing multi-factor data and is:

- Generally accepted and understood by
  management
- Supported by various software products
  from spreadsheet to advanced statistical
  analysis software

Regression analysis can be used to analyze varying and
complex information. Regression analysis creates a
mathematical model that can:

- Graphically depict the relationship of
  various data
- Include both quantitative and qualitative
  factors
- Calculate the relative importance of various
  factors in the model.

As valuable as regression analysis is, it can also lead to improper conclusions if not applied properly.

Da-Simple Sales Company was testing the theory that for each additional sales person hired profits will increase. Myron Simple was convinced that this was true because he had hired ten new salespeople in the last six months and sales had steadily risen.

Myron plotted the data on sales and number of salespeople and performed a simple regression analysis as depicted below in Figure 10-6.

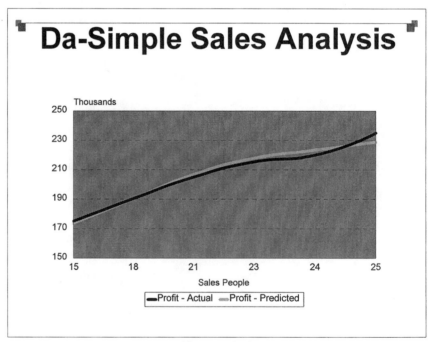

Figure 10-6

Example
(Continued)

The regression analysis showed an almost near linear regression. The correlation coefficient was 97% and Myron was convinced.

Without presenting his findings to senior management, Myron hired five additional salespeople the following month expecting profit to rise almost $30,000 based upon his regression formula.

As depicted in Figure 10-7, sales plummeted and profits were wiped out within two months. Myron was ordered to reanalyze the information and correct his actions.

Myron had not taken seasonal effects on sales or market saturation into consideration. Had Myron realized that the timing of the sales growth corresponded with the holiday season and sales traditionally decrease after Valentines Day his conclusions may have been different.

Even if the new salespeople did generate additional sales, the company would not have been able to absorb their salaries due to the seasonal decrease in sales.

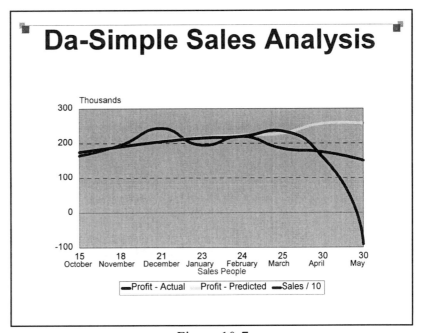

Figure 10-7

The previous example may be over-simplified, but it points out several considerations when using regression analysis:

- The number of data points and the time period over which data is taken have a great impact upon the reliability of the analysis.

- Factors other than past performance, such as market and economic conditions as well as seasonal effects, should be considered.

These considerations are also valid when analyzing gaps in performance. Companies in various industries may have different economic and market factors affecting performance.

Tips

✐ Regression analysis and stepwise regression can be used to determine the relative importance of various performance measures in a process. These measures can then be combined into a composite measure or index that can be measured and tracked over time.

✐ It is often useful to use more advanced statistical methods such as *time-series analysis and forecasting, design of experiments,* and *analysis of variance* to analyze complex data.

❺ **Modifying Best Practice for the Environment**

After a thorough analysis, the benchmarking team is ready to apply the information to its organization. Some process improvements will be relatively obvious and easily adapted to the company's work environment. These solutions should be implemented quickly and used to achieve short-term improvement goals.

Other facets of the competitive advantage may be linked to more complex factors or process enablers. For example, a gap may be caused by superior information systems and technologies that would take years to copy and would be outdated by the time they are implemented. In this case you need to look beyond the obvious solution and look at the underlying factors that are making the technology produce the superior results.

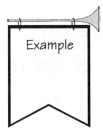

Example

Company A, a multinational service company with a dedicated sales force, was experiencing significant gains in market share. Its competitor, Company B, learned that a new computer system was providing the Company A sales staff with real-time information related to service capacity. Salespeople were receiving unsold services reports and selling those services at a discount. The theory was that the incremental revenue resulted in increased profitability as compared to the cost of idle capacity.

Although their information systems were less sophisticated, Company B also had useful capacity information. Company B combined its service capacity information with its superior contact management system. Unsold services were organized by service type and matched to the needs of its customers. The services were then sold at a discount, but at a higher margin than those of Company A.

Looking beyond the obvious to the process enablers allows you to use benchmarking to meet long-term goals. Long-term goals cannot be met by simply looking at short-term corrections. Looking beyond the current state, you can envision what the best practice will be in five years and create the enablers for the future.

Planning the improvement

At this point in the benchmarking process, the team returns to the basics of process improvement discussed in Chapters 4 and 7. By reexamining the internal process with the knowledge gained from benchmarking, the team should be able to develop new process improvement ideas.

Simple forms like the *Redesign Planning Form* shown in Table 10-4 are useful for focusing the redesign efforts of the benchmarking team.

Redesign Planning Form			
Suppliers		**Customers**	
Internal	External	Internal	External
Current Steps in Process:		**Ideal Steps in Process:**	
Knowledge/skills/abilities		Knowledge/skills/abilities	
Process/Plant/ Tools/resources/equipment		Process/Plant/ Tools/resources/equipment	

Table 10-4

Computer Modeling

One useful and increasingly popular tool is computer modeling. Computer modeling includes:

- Projection spreadsheets
- Regression models
- Object oriented modeling programs
- Flowcharting software that can manipulate performance indicators
- Graphical modeling software

Modeling software can be used to estimate the impact of a change in the process prior to implementation. For example, a spreadsheet can be used to calculate the return on investment for new information technology at multiple investment levels. The profit improvement can be modeled using regression analysis based upon the performance measures identified.

More sophisticated modeling technology can simulate the process and calculate the effects of process changes on performance. Various modeling programs of this sort are available for both manufacturing and service applications.

As in all computer applications, the model is only as good as its design and the data utilized in the simulation.

Implementation Phase

The implementation phase in a benchmarking project is the same as for any process redesign effort. The method for identifying potential improvements involved learning from others as opposed to looking only within the company.

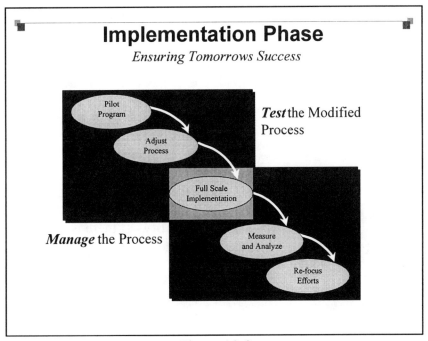

Figure 10-8

Whether benchmarking is more appropriate than the traditional internal approach depends upon the specific circumstances. Benchmarking will not be more effective if the company has not progressed down the learning curve of process improvement. Without the experience of internal process improvement, the benchmarking team may not have mastered the ability to understand its partner's processes.

The five steps of the implementation stage are discussed in detail in Chapter 2.

Benchmarking Ethics and Etiquette

Knowing the principles, ethics and etiquette of benchmarking contributes to effective benchmarking. Ethics and etiquette refer to more than just pleasantries and behavior. There are guidelines to ensure that benchmarking is fair and beneficial for all parties involved.

The American Society for Quality Control's Benchmarking Competency Center has promulgated several documents on benchmarking to assist companies performing benchmarking studies. Inherent in these documents are nine principles:

❶ Legality
❷ Exchange
❸ Confidentiality
❹ Use
❺ First Party Contact
❻ Third Party Contact
❼ Preparation
❽ Completion
❾ Understanding and Action

❶ **Legality** - If there is ever a question of whether something is legal, it probably is not.

Avoid action that may be considered a restraint of trade, price fixing, or bid rigging. When cost is an element of price, which it usually is, do not discuss cost issues with competitors.

Consider if information requested or shared may be deemed intellectual property. Intellectual property includes inventions, computer programs, designs and material that may lead to patents, service marks and similar intangible assets.

❷ **Exchange** - Be prepared and willing to share information equivalent or similar to that requested of your partner.

Ensure that you have the authority to share information with your partner. Either do not ask for something that you cannot provide, or inform your partner of the restriction before making the request.

Consider the company's culture and sensitivity when making information requests. Although you may be willing to exchange the information, they may not. The process by which the information is gathered or stored should be the aim of your information requests. Rarely is customer research, market studies or personnel information relevant to a benchmarking effort.

❸ **Confidentiality** - Do not divulge information received in a benchmarking effort without the prior consent of your benchmarking partner. Even the fact that the company is partnering with you may be confidential in their eyes.

Most organizations will require a confidentiality agreement restricting the use of proprietary information. Proprietary information is any information:

- Tangible or intangible;
- That was created, acquired or controlled by an organization; and
- That has not been published or released without restriction.

❹ **Use** - Use information obtained through benchmarking strictly for improving operations within the partnering organizations.

Information obtained should not be used to market or sell without the express consent of the parties. Using the results of a company's efforts in order to sell consulting services to a prospect or a client is unethical.

❺ **First Party Contact** - Determine who the appropriate person is within an organization and initiate contacts through that person.

Most large organizations who regularly conduct benchmarking studies have a designated contact. This contact can usually be obtained from the consortiums or consultants who provide benchmarking information.

Many companies have developed guidelines for benchmarking. Obtain mutual agreement on:

- the procedures to be followed; and
- the exchange of information.

❻ **Third Party Contact** - Obtain permission before providing an individual's name as a benchmarking contact. Do not provide contact information in a group discussion or other open forum without the contact's permission.

❼ **Preparation** - Demonstrate commitment to the efficiency and effectiveness of the benchmarking process by being adequately prepared.

Advance preparation is especially important at the initial contact with a prospective partner. Provide an agenda in advance and maintain focus on the benchmarking issues. Have information on your process with you and share it as appropriate to the discussion.

As a partner, request an advance copy of your questionnaire or work program so you can be prepared prior to the visit. Make the visit to your organization efficient by ensuring that the appropriate individuals will be available for your partner.

❽ **Completion** - Follow through on any commitment made during the benchmarking process in a timely manner. The goal of benchmarking is for both sides to receive a benefit from the exchange of information.

⑨ **Understanding and Action** - Obtain an understanding of how your benchmarking partner would like to be treated and act accordingly. Specifically:

- Always treat people with respect;
- Introduce all attendees at site visits and explain why they are present;
- Keep to the schedule on your agenda;
- Offer your partner a reciprocal visit; and
- Thank your partner for their time and effort.

Outcome

In undertaking a benchmarking project, many organizations are breaking the old paradigm

"If it wasn't developed here, it's no good."

Benchmarking is learning from others for competitive advantage. If you conduct benchmarking properly you will:

- Have a better understanding of how you do business;
- Learn more about competition, industry leaders, and your organization's environment;
- Create positive change. People will respond to clear and compelling information presented with management support; and
- Increase performance to such a level that others will seek you out.

CHAPTER 11

Keeping on Track

Process redesign success is anything but guaranteed. The entire notion of questioning the way an organization fulfills customer requirements and implementing necessary change is excruciating. Simply put, the entire change process is difficult and expensive. However, a payback of 5-10 times the required investment is not uncommon. The key to realizing these returns is to prudently consider the cost/benefit relationship of any potential project and to proceed with caution.

We are convinced that our philosophy of Process Redesign and Management produces the best results with minimal risk. Unlike wholesale clean-slate reengineering, we promote evaluating current business processes to determine the degree of change required and taking a scientific approach to bring about this change. Further, whether the required change is radical or incremental, we espouse the continuous management of processes by an ongoing monitoring of performance.

Like all change initiatives, our approach is not entirely risk-free and must be continually managed. It requires ongoing effort to keep the project focused and productive. If ignored or neglected, the project will invariably lose momentum and direction.

What follows are several "red flags" that can alert management or a redesign team that an effort is going astray and is less likely to deliver desired results. Fortunately, most of these obstacles to success are visible early on, so the problems can be corrected and dealt with decisively.

Lack of Communication

One of the most commonly overlooked and critical components of a successful process redesign project is the level of communication required, both among those directly involved and between the teams and the remainder of the organization, including management. Insufficient communication almost always retards the progress of the effort, often to the point of failure.

Regardless of whether the desired degree of change to a business process is a radical overhaul or incremental improvement, it is vital that an effective communication program be developed early and maintained throughout the process. Respondents to one survey regarding project communication cited the following ten aspects of communication as the most difficult to achieve, in order of difficulty:

- Getting across the magnitude of change
- Communicating frequently enough
- Responding to concerns about job restructuring and layoffs
- Using a common language and concepts understandable to all levels
- Responding to rumors
- Maintaining continuous visibility of reengineering "champion"
- Maintaining enthusiasm without being repetitious
- Maintaining a consistent message
- Devising a communication campaign
- Maintaining communication among team members

["Information Week," September 12, 1994]

Communication must be relentless. When it comes to process redesign, there is no such thing as over-communication. Virtually every team that undertakes redesign underestimates the amount of communication required; and, communication does not cease when implementation begins. The message must continue to be sent. Stopping prior to implementation could be interpreted as the end of executive commitment.

Communication can be made simple. Basic concepts must not be wrapped in fancy jargon. The motivation for process improvement must be expressed in terms accessible to everyone in the organization. We have found the following communication tools most widely used, in order of use:

- Small groups and team meetings

- Memoranda
- Large open meetings
- Newsletters
- E-mail
- Off-site events
- Voice mail
- Videotape

Each process redesign organization must adopt a communication program that works for them. There are probably accepted communication medium already in place in the company that should suffice. Regardless of the form chosen, it is imperative that communication among the teams, and with the remainder of the organization, be regular and consistent.

"Where's the CEO?"

Not only the CEO, but other members of the senior management team must remain personally and visibly involved throughout the initiative. How the senior management team spends their time is a powerful signal to the rest of the organization of the priority attached to a redesign effort. The CEO and other senior executives must be prepared to devote significant time to the initiative and become truly involved for most or all of its duration.

Lack of "Process" Orientation

Process Management must focus on redesigning a fundamental business process, not on departments or organizational units. We cannot overemphasize this point. Most businesspeople are not "process-oriented;" they are focused on tasks, on jobs, on people, on structures, but not on processes. However, the extent to which customers are satisfied with services and products is a direct result of the business process that delivers the services or products. To truly improve the ability to satisfy customers, you must understand and assess the capacity of processes to fulfill customer desires and expectations.

Redesigning Too Early

Forgoing an analysis of the current process and proceeding straight into redesign has a certain intuitive appeal. This is the essence of true reengineering--establishing a new business process with no consideration of how the existing process performs. This haste to jump to the redesign phase is particularly tempting to management who feel a sense of urgency about delivering a solution.

Yet, teams that invest time up front in order to understand how a current process performs and why shortfalls occur, report that this analysis proves invaluable in focusing attention on the critical issues during a redesign process. Such an analysis also gives the team early warning of the scale of change required, and begins to highlight likely resistance and organizational limitations that must be overcome in the redesign and change process.

"We've Identified 37 Core Processes in Our Business"

This is a strong danger signal that the effort has been inappropriately scoped. Typically, most businesses can be separated into three to five core processes. If there appear to be many more, the processes are probably being defined too narrowly and do not focus on the key output requirements. In breaking down their business into multitudes of core processes, organizations are likely to miss major opportunities for performance improvement, and the effort will run a much greater risk of dissipating through loss of focus.

Process Redesign & Management: Beyond Reengineering
© 1995 Windham Brannon Business Advisory Services, LLC

Quitting Too Early

It is not surprising to hear that some companies abandon process redesign or scale back their goals at the first sign of a problem. They lose their nerve. Others call off their effort at the first sign of success. As soon as they have something to show for all their time and effort, they stop. The initial success becomes an excuse to return to business as usual. In either case, by failing to persevere the company forgoes the potential huge payoff.

Placing Prior Constraints on the Scope of the Effort

A redesign effort is doomed to fail when, before it even begins, management narrowly defines the problem to be solved or limits the scope of the effort. Defining the problem and establishing scope are steps in the redesign effort itself. Successful process redesign and management begins with articulating the objectives that the effort seeks to achieve, not the ways in which these objectives will be met.

It is also common for senior management, because of their extensive experience with the company or knowledge of the process being examined, to use the work of the improvement teams to merely validate preconceived notions as to causes of poor performance. These individuals may also feel they know the solutions to the problem and how they should be implemented.

While these members of management possess invaluable insight into the process, if this occurs the team will feel powerless and uninspired. They will feel that they have no influence over identifying problems and proposing solutions. They will feel that the team exists solely to justify management's opinions of performance problems.

Too Many Redesign Efforts Going on Simultaneously

Process Redesign and Management requires sharp focus and enormous discipline, which is another way of saying that companies must concentrate their efforts on only a few processes at any given time. An organization becomes bewildered rather than energized when it is asked to do too much at once. Although customer service, research and development, and sales all need improvement, nothing is likely to happen if a company tries to tackle them all at once unless it has exceptional management capacity. Management's time and attention are limited, and process redesign will not obtain the crucial support it needs if managers must float among projects.

Lack of Emphasis on Implementation

Process Management is not just about redesign. It is also about translating new designs and ideas into reality. The difference between process management winners and losers does not usually lie in the quality of their ideas and techniques. With the winners, the results of the problem identification and resolution phases of the effort are successfully implemented and incorporated into the business process. They know how to leverage early success in analysis and redesign into a new, high performance business process or subprocess.

Lack of Necessary Resources

Process Redesign and Management requires a significant investment by the organization. The most important component of this investment is the devotion of time and attention by the company's best performers, including senior management. Improvement team members must be given the time necessary to attend meetings and work on the project. The improvement effort must be as high on their list of priorities as their routine job functions and responsibilities.

Process Redesign and Management must be the personal project of the CEO or other senior management members. They must commit regular effort in guiding and monitoring the activities of all redesign projects underway in the organization. Assigning inadequate resources to the effort also sends signals to the company that management does not consider the endeavor to be important and encourages people to ignore or resist it in the expectation that before long it will have run its course and dissipate.

If companies do not put process redesign at the top of their agenda, they should leave it off entirely. If management attention and effort are spread across many different management projects, of which redesign is only one, redesign will not get the intense attention it requires. Without constant management input, resistance and inertia will bring the effort to a halt.

Redesigning Processes Too Slowly

The time elapsing between initiating Process Redesign and Management and having some benefit to show for the effort should not exceed nine months. This does not mean that the entire redesigned process must be implemented within nine months, nor does it mean that the new process be rolled out to the entire organization within this time frame. It simply means that enough of the redesigned process should be operating at a higher performance level so that you can point to it as proof that the new design will actually work in the real world.

Within nine months of initiating the project, you must develop an understanding of the old process, come up with your conceptualization of the redesigned process, test the new process design in a pilot, and implement parts of it in the real world.

Once full-scale implementation begins, between ⅓ and ½ of the expected total performance improvement should be deliverable in the first 12 months of implementation. Thus, within 21 to 24 months of the project initiation, you should plan on having implemented the new, redesigned process and it should deliver up to one-half of the promised benefit. Any less, and the project runs the risk of being considered a drag on company resources.

In other words, you must do a tremendous amount of work in a short period of time. However, the alternative is failure and status quo. If you allow process redesign to drag on for too long, it will die. Upper management will lose faith and begin to withdraw its funding, since alternative programs are competing for these resources. Also, the resisters will have more time to dig in their heels.

Waiting until Process Redesign and Management implementation is underway before discovering mistakes or oversights in these areas is unacceptably risky. It may be too late to recover, rethink, and launch a second effort. The challenge is to recognize, at every stage in the process, the warning signals that desired performance improvements may not be on course for delivery. Or, put more positively, the challenge is to navigate successfully around the many pitfalls, and to keep tightly focused on the distinctive value that Process Redesign and Management will add.

Appendices

Process Assessment Ratings and Criteria

5. The process, as currently practiced, is ineffective; major exposures exist requiring expeditious, corrective actions. The basics of quality management are not in place.

4. The process, as currently practiced, has some operational and/or control weaknesses which require corrective action, but the resulting exposures are containable, and the weaknesses can be corrected in the near future. The basics of quality management are in place.

3. The process, as currently practiced, is effective and no significant operational effectiveness or control exposures exist. Substantial quality improvement activity is in progress. Defect-free criteria has been established.

2. In addition to Category 3 requirements, major improvements (including simplification) have been made to the process with tangible and measurable results realized. Business direction is evaluated with resulting process changes anticipated and committed.

1. In addition to Category 2 requirements, the outputs of the process are assessed by the owner and the auditor, from the customer's viewpoint, as being substantially defect-free (i.e., to the level the process can reasonably deliver), and no significant operational inefficiencies are anticipated.

Process Rating Characteristics

5.   A process is rated (5) if any of the following conditions exist:
    1.   The process does not achieve intended results (does not get the job done).
    2.   The process has major control exposures (i.e., potential cause of material business disruption) requiring expeditious corrective actions.
    3.   The process is not defined, ownership is unclear, and key measurements are not in place.

4.   A process is rated (4) if it exhibits all of the following characteristics:
    1.   The process generally achieves intended results(gets the job done), but some operational exposures exist; however, these exposures:
        •   Are containable.
        •   Have been documented to management.
        •   Have established action plans in place.
        •   Have near-term resolution dates.

    2.   Controls have been assessed and some significant control exposures (i.e., separation of duties, data integrity, asset protection) have been identified; however, all identified exposures:
        •   Are contained.
        •   Have been documented to management.
        •   Have established action plans in place.
        •   Have near term resolution dates.

    3.   The basics of Process Management are in place:
        •   Process is defined.
        •   Process is fully documented.
        •   Ownership has been assigned and acknowledged.
        •   Control measurements have been established
        •   Key indicators are in place and are being tracked

---

Process Rating Characteristics (Cont.)

3.   A process is rated (3) if it demonstrated <u>all</u> (4) rating traits and in addition, exhibits all of the following characteristics:

1.   The process is consistently effective at current volume/complexity level, and no significant operational exposures exist.

2.   No significant control exposures exist:
- Data integrity is verified.
- Adequate separation of duties exists.
- Assets are protected and verified regularly.
- Transactions are executed with management authorization.
- Adequate supporting procedures are in place.

3.   Quality Management has progressed:
- Defect-free criteria (long term objective) has been established for the process.
- Process quality is being monitored against the defect-free criteria.
- Quality improvement activities have been initiated and documented with action plans and target dates.

2.   A process is rated (2) when it achieves <u>all</u> (3) rating traits plus the following:

1.   Major process improvements have been achieved with measurable results as demonstrated by an improving defect trend.

2.   Efficiency gains are being realized:
- Process simplification.
- Unnecessary work eliminated.
- Reduced resources.

Appendix A
Process Rating System

Process Rating Characteristics (Cont.)

1.   A process is rated (1) when it achieves the following in addition to <u>all</u> of the above characteristics:
    1.   Defect-free level achieved and sustained.
    2.   Process operates with minimum resources.
    3.   Process can handle a reasonable level of additional volume and/or complexity.
    4.   Further investment in process improvement is not justified.
    5.   Substantial customer satisfaction is achieved.

Process Rating Characteristics (Cont.)

1. Answer Checklist Questions YES or NO:
    a. Supporting tests and reviews should be conducted to determine if the process owner can answer each question yes or no.
    b. Any favorable response (YES) should be supported by documentation. This documentation may be requested when the ratings are revised.

2. Determine the Process Rating:
    a. Process Ratings begin at 5 and go to 1, with 1 being the highest rating (Defect-free).
    b. Your process should be rated the same as the highest category in which it achieves 100% favorable (YES) answers to the assessment checklist. The process must demonstrate all characteristics of a rating level to achieve that rating.
    c. Process Ratings are <u>cumulative</u>. A higher rating can only be achieved by meeting <u>all</u> requirements of that category and <u>all</u> previous categories. Ratings are <u>not</u> weighted average of favorable answers from all categories.
    d. If a process cannot answer all questions in category 4 favorably, it should be rated a 5.

3. Communicate your results:
    a. Complete the last page of the Process Assessment Checklist and sign (must be signed by process owner).
    b. Forward your completed checklist to the reviewer.

Process Rating Characteristics (Cont.)

Process: _____
Owner: _____

(4) rating is achieved when questions 1-14 below can be answered favorably:

1. Does the process generally achieve the intended results? (Does it get the job done?)

2. If operational exposures exist, are they contained and have they been documented to management?

3. Have action plans and near-term target dates been established for all operational exposures?

4. Have the key control elements of the process been tested?

5. If significant control exposures exist, are they contained and have they been documented to management?

6. Have action plans and near-term target dates been established for all control exposures?

7. Has the process been defined?

8. Has an owner been assigned?

9. Does the owner understand and accept his/her responsibility for the quality and control of the process?

10. Has the Quality Improvement Program been communicated to employees involved in the process?

Process Assessment Checklist

Process: _____

Owner: _____

(4) rating is achieved when questions 1 -14 below can be answered favorably:

11.   Is the process documentation complete (flowcharts, subprocess, linkage, etc)?

12.   Have control measurements been identified?

13.   Have key indicators with quantative objectives been established?

14.   Are the key indicators tracked, documented, and reviewed by the process owner monthly?

Process Assessment Checklist

Process: _____
Owner: _____

(3) rating is achieved when questions 15-28 below can be answered favorably in addition to questions 1 -14.

15.   Does the current level of process operation indicate that the process will be consistently effective given the current volume/complexity level?

16.   Are all documented operational exposures insignificant to the effective functioning of the process?

17.   Are all documented control concerns insignificant to the effective functioning of the process and the overall process control posture?

18.   Has the date integrity of the process been sample tested and verified?

19.   Where application systems provide information, do they contain adequate and verifiable controls to ensure the integrity of their results?

20.   Is there adequate separation of duties within the process?

21.   Are assets safeguarded and regularly verified to the financial records?

22.   Are all process transactions executed with management authorization?

Process Assessment Checklist

Process: _____
Owner: _____

(3) rating is achieved when questions 15 - 28 below can be answered favorably in addition to questions 1 -14:

23.   Are procedures in place to clearly communicate process control requirements?

24.   Has defect-free criteria been established?

25.   Is process quality being monitored against defect-free criteria?

26.   Have quality improvement activities been initiated?

27.   Have owners identified Key Personnel who are trained in the application of process analysis techniques or equivalent?

28.   Are the quality improvement activities fully documented with action plans and target dates?

Process Assessment Checklist

Process: _____
Owner: _____

(2) rating is achieved when questions 29 - 34 below can be answered favorably in addition to questions 1 - 28:

29.   As a result of Quality Management, have major improvements to the process been achieved with measurable results?

30.   Is the defect trend improving?

31.   Are measurements in place to determine resource utilization?

32.   Have efficiency gains been achieved (resources reduced)?

33.   Has the process been simplified?

34.   Have unnecessary process steps been eliminated (rework, expediting, exception handling, etc.)?

Process Assessment Checklist

Process: _____
Owner: _____

(1)rating is achieved when questions 35 - 40 below can be answered favorably in addition to questions 1 - 35.

35. Has the desired defect-free level been reached and sustained?

36. Is the process efficient in that it operates with minimum resources?

37. Can the process handle a reasonable level of additional volume and/or complexity without being strained? (Is the process flexible?)

38. Are measurements in place to determine process capacity (volume and capacity)?

39. Is further investment in process improvement not justified?

40. Has substantial customer satisfaction been achieved?

Process Assessment Checklist

Process: _____
Owner: _____

As a result of my reviews and tests, and the completion of a Process Assessment Checklist (attached), I have rated my process as _____.

                                    Signed _____

                                              Owner

Process Assessment Checklist

Process: _____
Owner: _____

(1)rating is achieved when questions 35 - 40 below can be answered favorably in addition to questions 1 - 35.

35.   Has the desired defect-free level been reached and sustained?

36.   Is the process efficient in that it operates with minimum resources?

37.   Can the process handle a reasonable level of additional volume and/or complexity without being strained? (Is the process flexible?)

38.   Are measurements in place to determine process capacity (volume and capacity)?

39.   Is further investment in process improvement not justified?

40.   Has substantial customer satisfaction been achieved?

Appendix A
Process Rating System

Process Assessment Checklist

Process: _____

As a result of my reviews and tests, and the completion of a Process Assessment Checklist (attached), I have rated my process as _____.

Signed _____

Owner

Bibliography

Books

Bemowski, Karen. *Inside the Baldrige Award Criteria* (Milwaukee, WI, ASQC Quality Press, 1993).

Berkowitz, Leonard. *A Survey of Social Psychology 2nd Ed.* (Holt Rinehart and Winston, 1980) .

Bogan, Christopher E. and English, Michael J. *Benchmarking for Best Practices* (McGraw Hill, 1994).

Camp, Robert C. *Benchmarking: The Search for Industry Best Practices that Lead to Superior Performance* (Milwaukee, WI, ASQC Quality Press, 1989).

Camp, Robert C. *Business Process Benchmarking - Finding and Implementing Best Practices* (Milwaukee, WI, ASQC Quality Press, 1995).

Carr, David K., et.al., *BreakPoint Business Process Redesign* (Arlington, VA, Coopers & Lybrand, 1992).

Delta Airlines, *Leadership Development* (1993).

Deming, W. Edwards. *Out of the Crisis* (Cambridge, MA, Massachusetts Institute of Technology, 1986).

Galloway, Dianne. *Mapping Work Processes* (Milwaukee, WI, ASQC Quality Press, 1994).

Hammer, Michael, and Champy, James. *Reengineering the Corporation: A Manifesto for Business Revolution.* (New York : Harper Collins, 1993).

Hammer, Michael and Stanton, Steven. Reprints from "Fortune" May 15, 1995. pp 105-114 of *The Reengineering Revolution.* (Hammer and Co., 1995).

Joint Commission on Accreditation of Healthcare Organizations, *An Introduction to Quality Improvement In Healthcare: The Transition from QA to CQI* (Oakbrook Terrace, IL, JCAHO, 1992).

Joint Commission on Accreditation of Healthcare Organizations, *Using Quality Improvement Tools in a Health Care Setting.* (Oakbrook Terrace, IL, JCAHO, 1992).

Juran, J.M, *Juran on Leadership for Quality: An Executive Handbook.* (New York, NY: The Free Press, 1989)

Lynch, Robert F. and Werner, Thomas J. *Continuous Improvement: Teams and Tools* (Atlanta, GA, Qualteam Inc., 1992).

Malcolm Baldrige National Quality Award - 1994 Award Criteria (Gaithersburg, MD: United States Department of Commerce, Technology Administration, National Institute of Standards and Technology).

Malcolm Baldrige National Quality Award - 1995 Award Criteria (Gaithersburg, MD: United States Department of Commerce, Technology Administration, National Institute of Standards and Technology).

Marsh, S. et al. *Facilitating and Training in Quality Function Deployment* (Methuen, MA: GOAL/QPC, 1991).

Mendenhall, William and McClave, James T., *A Second Course in Business Statistics: Regression Analysis* (San Francisco, CA, Dellen Publishing Company, 1981).

Miller, Lawrence A. et al. *Whole System Architecture: Beyond Reengineering: Designing the High Performance Organization* (Atlanta, GA, The Miller Consulting Group, 1994).

Montgomery, Douglas C. *Statistical Quality Control 2nd Edition* (John Wiley & Sons, 1991).

Montgomery, Douglas C., and Peck, Elizabeth A., *Introduction to Linear Regression Analysis, 2nd Ed.*, (John Wiley & Sons, 1992).

Morse, Wayne J., Roth, Harold P. and Poston, Kay M. *Measuring, Planning, and Controlling Quality Costs* (Montvale, NJ: Institute of Management Accountants, 1987).

Roberts, Lon. *Process Reengineering: The Key to Achieving Breakthrough Success* (Milwaukee, WI, ASQC Quality Press, 1994).

Walton, Mary. *The Deming Management Method* (Putnam Publishing Co., New York, NY, 1986).

Watson, Gregory H. *The Benchmarking Workbook* (Cambridge, MA, Productivity Press, 1992).

Xerox Corporation, *Meeting Right™ Software Users Guide* (Rochester, NY, 1993).

Articles

Benchmarking Committee - Quality Management Division of ASQC. "Committee News and Highlights." *The Quality Management Forum* (Fall 1994 Volume 20, Number 3):15-17.

Browning, John. "The Power of Process Redesign: A Roundtable Discussion with Richard Hegate, Ron Laird and Greg Prang." *The McKinsey Quarterly* (1993 Number 1):47-58.

Caldwell, Bruce. "Missteps, Miscues." *Informationweek*, June 20, 1994. pp. 50-60.

Center for Video Education. "The Benchmarking Process." *Quality Management Report* Obtained through the Financial Management Network, May 1994

Czarnecki, Mark T. "Tips on Benchmarking From Industry Leaders." *Newsletter of the AICPA Consulting Services Division*:6-8

Hagel, John III. "Keeping CPR on Track." *The McKinsey Quarterly* (1993 Number 1):59-72.

Hall, Gene, Rosenthal, Jim and Wade, Judy. "How to Make Reengineering Really Work." *Harvard Business Review* (November-December 1993): 119-131.

Hammer, Michael. "Reengineering Work: Don't Automate, Obliterate." *Harvard Business Review* 68 (July-August 1990):104-112.

Headgate, Richard. "Immoderate Redesign." *The McKinsey Quarterly* (1993 Number 1):73-88.

Hunter, Michael R., and Van Landingham, Richard D., "Listening to the Customer Using QFD." *Quality Progress*, (April 1994):55-59.

Johnson, Elizabeth D., "Re-engineering: Who, What, When, How, and How Much?" *The Quality Management Forum*, ASQC, Vol. 20, No. 2, (Summer 1994):11-14.

Kane, Edward J., "IBM's Quality Focus on the Business Process." *Quality Progress* (April, 1986): 24-33.

Knight, Robert M., "Reengineering: The Business Buzzword." *Sky* (January 1995): 22-28.

Mathews, Jay and Katel, Peter. "The Cost of Quality." *Newsweek* (September 7, 1992):48-49.

Port, Otis and Smith, Geoffrey. "Beg Borrow and Benchmark." *Business Week* (November 30, 1992): 74-75.

Schein, Lawrence, "The Road to Total Quality: Views of Industry Experts." *The Conference Board* (Research Bulletin No. 233): 1-17.

Simmerman, Scot J., "Achieving Service Quality Improvements." *Quality Progress*, (November 1993):47-50.

Smith, Baker A., "Reengineering the Family Firm." *Family Business* (Autumn 1994): 32-38.

Stewart, Thomas A., "Reengineering: The Hot New Management Tool." *Fortune* (August 23, 1993):41-48.

Appendix B
Bibliography

Stewart, Thomas A., "GE Keeps Those Ideas Coming." *Fortune* (August 12, 1991):41-49.

Swanson, Roger. "Quality Benchmark Deployment." *Quality Progress* (December 1993):81-83.

Treece, James B, "QUALITY: Small and Midsize Companies Seize the Challenge - Not a Moment Too Soon." *Business Week* (November 30, 1992):67-71.

Wilson, Linda, "New Ways to Rebuild Business." *Informationweek* (September 5, 1994):50-58.

Wozniak, Christopher, "Proactive vs. Reactive SPC." *Quality Progress*, (February 1994):49-50.

Yang, Dori Jones, "When the Going Gets Tough, Boeing Gets Touchy-Feely." *Business Week* (January 17, 1994):65-67.

Index

About the Authors

Doug Montgomery is a professor of industrial and management systems engineering at Arizona State University since 1988, received his B.S., M.S. and Ph.D. degrees from Virginia Polytechnic Institute, all in engineering. From 1969 to 1984 he was on the faculty of the School of Industrial & Systems Engineering at the Georgia Institute of Technology, and from 1984 to 1988 he was at the University of Washington, where he held the John M. Fluke Distinguished Chair of Manufacturing Engineering, was professor of mechanical engineering, and director of the program in industrial engineering.

In addition to his work in process redesign and improvement, Dr. Montgomery has interests in quality engineering, experimental design, regression modeling and time series analysis, and the application of operations research methodology to problems in manufacturing systems. He has authored and co-authored many technical papers in these fields and is an author of ten other books. Dr. Montgomery is a Fellow of the American Society for Quality Control, a Senior Member of the Institute of Industrial Engineers, a Senior Member of the Operations Research Society of America, a Senior Member of the Society of Manufacturing Engineers, and a Member of the American Statistical Association.

Sid Johnson is President of Windham Brannon Business Advisory Services, LLC, and an Executive Officer of Windham Brannon, PC., CPAs in Atlanta, Georgia. He received his B.S. degree in Accounting from the University of Kentucky and a Masters degree from Georgia State University. For the past twelve years he has worked with a diverse client base, including firms in manufacturing, distribution, real estate development and operations, professional services, food services, utilities and government agencies. His areas of concentration consist of all aspects of business process improvement and redesign, business and tax planning, and the restructuring of business entities to improve competitiveness.

He has conducted educational courses on a variety of topics of interest to CPAs and business people and has facilitated teams assembled to bring about positive change within companies of all sizes. He is a member of the American Institute of CPAs, Georgia Society of CPAs, American Society of Quality Control and American Society of Training and Development.

Gary Feldman is a principal of Windham Brannon Business Advisory Services, LLC. He received his B.S. and Masters degrees in Accounting from the University of Florida. Since 1986 he has been assessing, designing and redesigning financial management, information and operational systems. One of his specialities is the evaluation, selection, customization and implementation of financial accounting software for companies of various sizes. He has a broad base of clients in service, utility, real estate, food services and manufacturing industries.

Mr. Feldman has lectured and published articles on diverse business and quality topics including activity based costing, benchmarking, continuous quality improvement, performance measurement and reengineering. He is a member of the AICPA, ASQC, Georgia Society of CPAs, Florida Institute of CPAs, and Institute of Management Accountants.

Order Form

Please send the following books:

	Qty	Each	Total
☐ Montgomery, D.C., J.S. Johnson and G.J. Feldman, *Process Redesign & Management: Beyond Reengineering*, Windham Brannon Business Advisory Services, LLC (Atlanta, GA, 1996)	____	$50	____
☐ Hines, W.W. and D.C. Montgomery, *Probability and Statistics in Engineering and Management Science, 3rd Ed.*, John Wiley & Sons (New York, 1990)	____	$75	____
☐ Montgomery, D.C., *Design and Analysis of Experiments, 3rd Ed.*, John Wiley & Sons (New York, 1991)	____	$75	____
☐ Johnson, L.A. and D.C. Montgomery, *Operations Research in Production Planning, Scheduling, and Inventory Control*, John Wiley & Sons (New York, 1974)	____	$65	____
☐ Montgomery, D.C. and E.A. Peck, *Introduction to Linear Regression Analysis, 2nd Ed.*, John Wiley & Sons (New York, 1992)	____	$55	____
☐ Montgomery, D.C., *Introduction to Statistical Quality Control, 2nd Ed.*, John Wiley & Sons (New York, 1991)	____	$65	____
☐ Montgomery, D.C., L.A. Johnson and J.S. Gardiner, *Forecasting and Time Series Analysis, 2nd Ed.*, McGraw-Hill (New York, 1990)	____	$65	____
☐ Montgomery, D.C. and G.C. Runger, *Applied Statistics and Probability for Engineers*, John Wiley & Sons (New York, 1994)	____	$65	____
☐ Myers, R.H. and D.C. Montgomery, *Response Surface Methodology: Process and Product Optimization with Designed Experiments*, John Wiley & Sons, (New York, 1995)	____	$55	____
☐ Please send me information on seminars/courses	____		____
Total			____

Mail your order to:

Windham Brannon Business Advisory Services, LLC
1355 Peachtree Street, NE, Suite 200
Atlanta, Georgia 30309
or call (404) 898-2001

Fax your order to: (404) 898-2010

On-line orders to: WBPCATL@aol.com or GJFWBPC@aol.com
Ask about quantity discounts.

Payment:
    Please send check or money order. Prices subject to change without notification. For latest prices call (404) 898-2001.

Name_____   Company_____
Title_____   Address_____
City, State, Zip_____   Phone _____Fax_____

Order Form

Please send the following books:

	Qty	Each	Total
❑ Montgomery, D.C., J.S. Johnson and G.J. Feldman, *Process Redesign & Management: Beyond Reengineering*, Windham Brannon Business Advisory Services, LLC (Atlanta, GA, 1996)	____	$50	____
❑ Hines, W.W. and D.C. Montgomery, *Probability and Statistics in Engineering and Management Science, 3rd Ed.*, John Wiley & Sons (New York, 1990)	____	$75	____
❑ Montgomery, D.C., *Design and Analysis of Experiments, 3rd Ed.*, John Wiley & Sons (New York, 1991)	____	$75	____
❑ Johnson, L.A. and D.C. Montgomery, *Operations Research in Production Planning, Scheduling, and Inventory Control*, John Wiley & Sons (New York, 1974)	____	$65	____
❑ Montgomery, D.C. and E.A. Peck, *Introduction to Linear Regression Analysis, 2nd Ed.*, John Wiley & Sons (New York, 1992)	____	$55	____
❑ Montgomery, D.C., *Introduction to Statistical Quality Control, 2nd Ed.*, John Wiley & Sons (New York, 1991)	____	$65	____
❑ Montgomery, D.C., L.A. Johnson and J.S. Gardiner, *Forecasting and Time Series Analysis, 2nd Ed.*, McGraw-Hill (New York, 1990)	____	$65	____
❑ Montgomery, D.C. and G.C. Runger, *Applied Statistics and Probability for Engineers*, John Wiley & Sons (New York, 1994)	____	$65	____
❑ Myers, R.H. and D.C. Montgomery, *Response Surface Methodology: Process and Product Optimization with Designed Experiments*, John Wiley & Sons, (New York, 1995)	____	$55	____
❑ Please send me information on seminars/courses	____		____
Total			____

Mail your order to:

Windham Brannon Business Advisory Services, LLC
1355 Peachtree Street, NE, Suite 200
Atlanta, Georgia 30309
or call (404) 898-2001

Fax your order to: (404) 898-2010

On-line orders to: WBPCATL@aol.com or GJFWBPC@aol.com
Ask about quantity discounts.

Payment:
    Please send check or money order. Prices subject to change without notification. For latest prices call (404) 898-2001.

Name_____   Company_____
Title_____   Address_____
City, State, Zip_____   Phone _____Fax_____